D1474857

SUSANNA DICKINSON
MESSENGER OF THE ALAMO

BY C. RICHARD KING

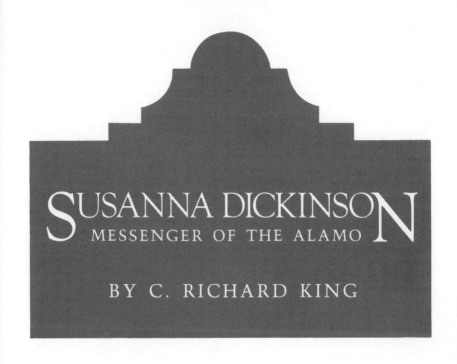

SUSANNA DICKINSON
MESSENGER OF THE ALAMO

BY C. RICHARD KING

COVER BY DON COLLINS

SHOAL CREEK PUBLISHERS, INC.
P.O. BOX 9737   AUSTIN, TEXAS 78766

PUBLISHED BY

SHOAL CREEK PUBLISHERS, INC.
P. O. BOX 9737, AUSTIN, TEXAS 78766

FIRST EDITION

LITHOGRAPHED AND BOUND IN THE UNITED STATES OF AMERICA

Library of Congress Cataloging in Publication Data
King, Clyde Richard.
Susanna Dickinson: Messenger of the Alamo.

Bibliography: p.
Includes index.
1. Dickenson, Susanna.   2. Alamo—Siege, 1836.
F390.D52K56   *976.4'03'0924 [B]*   *76-14814*
ISBN 0-88319-023-0

INTRODUCTION

When the idea of writing a biography of Susanna Dickinson first appealed, my feeling was that she was too well known as the woman at the Alamo, that collecting material on such a personality would involve reading libraries of printed works and leafing through reams and reams of brittle paper. A timid search proved otherwise; there was no great plethora of Dickinsoniana. The fact that she could neither read nor write assured historians that there would be none of her letters to her grandchildren, no answers written to questions raised by reporters lately learning of Alamo heroism, no recipes to reveal her secrets of making peach cobbler, no account books to show how she managed her boarding house, and no diaries or journals to tell of her life in early Texas.

Because of the shortage of first account materials, the author has welcomed family legends, many of them furnished by Willard Griffith Nitschke, a great granddaughter of Susanna. The author, too, has depended on Mrs. Nitschke for proper names; the variety of spellings is enough to give even the most experienced genealogist migraines.

The author has tried to be accurate and to label as such any surmises or assumptions; he also has been aware of the wide chasms of time that are void of explanation.

"DOUGHOREGAN"
STEPHENVILLE, TEXAS
2 MARCH 1976

C. Richard King

CONTENTS

ILLUSTRATIONS

SUSANNA DICKINSON

Angelina Dickinson
(Daughter of Susanna Dickinson)

Know all men, that we Almeron Dickinson

B D Johnson

All of the county of Hardeman, and State of Tennessee, are held and firmly bound unto the Governor of said State, for the time being, his successors in office, or assigns, in the sum of *twelve hundred and fifty Dollars,* which payment well and truly to be made, we bind ourselves our heirs, executors, and each and every of us and them, jointly, and severally, by these presents. Witness our hands and seals, this 24 th day of *May* 182 9

THE CONDITION OF THE ABOVE OBLIGATION IS SUCH, That whereas the above named Almeron Dickenson

Susanna Wilkerson hath this day prayed and obtained a license to marry

Now, if the said *Susanna* be an actual resident in the aforesaid county, and there shall not appear any lawful cause why the said Almeron Dickison & Susanna Wilkerson should not be joined together in Holy Matrimony as husband and wife: then this obligation to be void and of no effect; otherwise to remain in full force and virtue.

Almeron Dickinson (Seal)

B D Johnson (Seal)

ORIGINAL MARRIAGE LICENSE ISSUED TO SUSANNA WILKERSON AND ALMERON DICKINSON ON THE 24TH DAY OF MAY 1829. COURTESY OF MRS. R. E. NITSCHKE, GREAT GRANDDAUGHTER OF SUSANNA DICKINSON.

The rock house where Susanna and Joseph W. Hannig lived when they came to Austin still stands at 501 East Fifth Street.

THE J. W. HANNIG BUILDING (NOW DEMOLISHED) LOCATED ON PECAN STREET (NOW SIXTH) BETWEEN BRAZOS AND SAN JACINTO.

THE ALAMO, FROM ORIGINAL PAINTING MADE IN 1839 BY WILLIAM BISSEL. COURTESY ALAMO LIBRARY, DAUGHTERS OF THE REPUBLIC OF TEXAS

THE ALAMO—1976. PHOTOGRAPH BY ZINTGRAFF, SAN ANTONIO, TEXAS.

THE 1976 MONUMENT

Prior to the Texas Centennial, 1936, Almeron Dickinson Griffith was approached concerning the removal of the body of his grandmother, Susanna Wilkerson Dickinson, from Oakwood Cemetery, Austin, to rest with other Texas notables in the State Cemetery. He adamantly rejected such proposals.

Susanna's great granddaughter, Mrs. R. E. Nitschke, Jr., upheld her father's wishes, but she believed that the messenger of the Alamo deserved a monument in the state cemetery, so she campaigned for the Texas Legislature to recognize Susanna with a marker. Mrs. Nitschke's dreams were realized, and 140 years after Susanna Dickinson and her small child left a stilled Alamo to face Santa Anna, on March 6, 1976, a granite marker shaped like the state of Texas was unveiled by A. Stasswender. A bronze plaque in the outline of the Alamo, superimposed on the granite, reads:

Susanna Dickinson

1814 Hannig 1883

Her name belongs to Texas history. She cast her lot with the immortal heroes of the Alamo. After its fall, with the ''Babe'' in her arms, she carried the news to Gen. Sam Houston at Gonzales.

A chilling mist fell during dedication services. Charles Sumners, rector emeritus of St. David's Episcopal Church, Austin, gave an invocation, and when State Representative Sarah Weddington was unable to attend, Vicki Clark, a staff member, represented her and presented a brief outline of the role women have played in Texas history. Dr. C. Richard King, professor of journalism, The University of Texas, Austin, described the life of Susanna Dickinson, and Mrs. Nitschke told of her dream that her great grandmother be honored with a monument in the State Cemetery.

Services for the unveiling were under the direction of Ann Pollard Arthur, president of the Texian chapter, Daughters of the Republic of Texas.

MRS. R. E. NITSCHKE, Jr. BESIDE THE 1976 MONUMENT.

On Sunday, Oct. 7, 1883, Susanna Dickinson Hannig died, and two days later, her body was laid to rest in Oakwood Cemetery, Austin. Joseph W. Hannig ordered a white marble marker. For inscription details, see pages 117-118.

One of Hannig's nephews, E. A. Masur of Lockhart, during the Texas Centennial, 1936, began a crusade to have the state place a marker at Susanna's final resting place. Masur did not live to see his crusade completed, but on March 2, 1949, the State of Texas unveiled a slab of white marble covering the grave.

CHAPTER ONE

TENNESSEE YEARS

THE man, muscular from work at the anvil — gave his cupreous hand and she sprang into the sidesaddle. He tied her small valise to the horn then vaulted into the saddle on his own mount. The two on horseback waved to the girl's mother and father and to the passel of assorted young ones clustered in front of the log house,[1] some barefoot, all in homespun; and the children's delighted good-byes rang long after the riders had disappeared into the greening timber.

Any occasion that would bring together in friendship the settlers scattered at wide intervals over this newly tamed frontier of western Tennessee was something for the young people to anticipate, separated as they were from anybody but close kin by what must have seemed endless stretches of oak, hickory and tupelo — a log-rolling, a corn-husking, a quilting, even a camp meeting, but especially a wedding, the most frolicsome of all events. The children, excited over the prospect of this wedding, stole glances at the man who had come to fetch their sister. Almeron Dickinson. Until a few weeks earlier, he had courted their sister, and now Susanna Wilkerson was preparing to ride away with him — not as a bride but as a bridesmaid.

Almeron Dickinson. Years of smithing had toned his muscles and months of farriering under last summer's sun had burnished his skin until it still glistened like metal. His speech was distinct — touched with proof of his Pennsylvania birth and youth — in contrast with the traces of deep South that characterized the speech of others in the neighborhood.

Poor Susanna. She had previously had her chance to nab the blacksmith. He had called on her for months, but the courting had ended in a spat. And now, Susanna had agreed to serve as a bridesmaid at his wedding. The entire Wilkerson family was in front of the cabin to wave a farewell to her. Almeron would escort her to the house of the bride's father, and there Susanna would spend the night, admire the bridal finery, laugh with friends and help prepare for the wedding feast. Almeron would ride to Bolivar, the county seat, to take out the marriage bond and apply for the license.

Such a scene—of lighthearted leave-taking—a young woman and her escort saying goodbye to her family on the eve of a festive occasion — was nothing uncommon on the frontier. But, this particular scene had consequences few neighbors could have foretold, consequences which would move a pair of lovers to turn their backs forever on familiar ground and to leap from the rim of civilization, as they had known Tennessee, into the dark, the unknown — Texas.

Details of what happened during that ride between the Wilkerson farm and the village of Bolivar are now lost. Somewhere along the way, Almeron and Susanna changed their minds, deciding they were meant for each other. Of the jilted bride-elect, nothing is known — not even her name, nor by what wiles she had lured Almeron from Susanna. Nor her reason for choosing Susanna to be her bridesmaid. Somehow, there has crept into the story the intimation that the bride-to-be was a designing woman, one ''more to be censured than pitied.'' The legend, however, has come through Susanna's family.

Susanna was barely fifteen years old, a simple country girl who had not learned how to read or write—nothing unusual, for there were no schools, except private ones in the towns. And it would have been foolish for a poor man to lay out good money for a girl's education when her mother could teach her everything she would ever need to know. Susanna could sew a neat stitch, and the meals she prepared were as appetizing as any spread north of New Orleans.

Whatever Almeron's reasons for changing his mind as he and Susanna rode through the woods, they must have resulted from careful reasoning. He was no ephebus, liable to be dashed away by a whim or emotion, but a full grown, responsible man nearing thirty years of age, a Mason[2] and a former artilleryman in the United States Army. He was a registered voter in 1828 and 1829, and the few recorded facts of his later life show that he frequently was selected by his fellowmen to perform tasks requiring a man as reliable as the iron he forged into horseshoes. He often volunteered for acts that called for a courageous man. And historians note that in an age of romanticism, when posturing and hyperbole were in style, Dickinson never said or wrote a word that was not strictly necessary and pertinent to the action at hand.

Perhaps never in the short life remaining to him did he do a more courageous thing than he did that May day in the year, 1829, in Bolivar, Tennessee. Not when he went out in pursuit of murderous Comanche Indians, not when he fired one of the opening shots of the Texas Revolution nor when he faced certain death in the Alamo.

A month earlier, Dickinson had ridden into Bolivar, looking over the public square that some citizens claimed was an eyesore, glanced over the unpainted frame business houses that these same citizens declared detracted from ''the beauty'' of the community, and mentally he tried to picture the brick wall that some residents urged be erected around the entire square. Dickinson signed as security a note for John F. Robertson, who borrowed money from Edward Fitzhugh. When payment was not made, both Robertson and Dickinson had been called before Francis Shoemaker, justice of the peace. It was a relieved Dickinson who heard Robertson vow he would pay ''the fifty dollars 26 cents and costs of debt.'' The attorney representing Fitzhugh was Thomas J. Hardeman.[3]

On May 24, 1829, Dickinson again was in the public square of Bolivar. He tied the horses to the hitching post and helped Susanna from her saddle; together they entered the office of the county clerk, Thomas J. Hardeman. Almeron recognized the man behind the wooden desk as one who had served as attorney in the note case.

Hardeman completed the form for Dickinson, authorizing any ''Minister of the Gospel, having the care of souls, or to any Justice of the Peace'' of Hardeman County to perform the rites of matrimony between Almeron Dickerson and Susanna Wilkerson ''provided always that the Susanna be an actual resident of the aforesaid county of Hardeman.''

When the document was completed and in hand, Susanna and Almeron scanned it:

That whereas the above named Almeron Dickerson hath this day prayed and obtained a license to marry Susanna Wilkerson, Now, if the said Susanna be an actual resident in the aforesaid county, and there shall not appear any lawful cause why the said Almeron Dickinson & Susanna Wilkerson should not be joined together in Holy matrimony as husband and wife: then this obligation to be void and of no effect. . . .[4]

Appearing before the justice of the peace that same day, Susanna and Almeron pledged their marriage vows.

Mr. and Mrs. Almeron Dickinson probably set up housekeeping near the line separating Hardeman and Fayette Counties. A man named Dickinson operated a store in or near the little town of Kokomo, and it is possible that the couple settled near him, or they may have gone to Fayette or Haywood Counties.[5]

Almeron probably experienced no difficulty in getting work, for he could make axes, hoes, plowshares or cowbells. As a farrier, he knew how to shoe horses and oxen, and he frequently was consulted about the disease of cattle. He could pull an aching tooth if a neighbor demanded such service. And Susanna may have contributed to the family finances by keeping a boarder.[6]

The Dickinsons' stay in Hardeman County, Tennessee, was of short duration. Events were happening in Texas which would prepare the way for the family's seeking a new home.

CHAPTER TWO

GONZALES

EVEN before his grant was in hand, empresario Green DeWitt, confident that the Mexican government would approve his petition for locating settlers in Texas, appointed James Kerr[1] surveyor. With six other men, the homely Kerr galloped into Texas in search of the ideal location for the capital of the future colony. On a small, clear stream they named Kerr's Creek, approximately two and a half miles east of a junction of the San Marcos and Guadalupe rivers, these pioneers began building cabins. In early autumn, they were joined by the family of Francis Berry. While the area was filled with the sound of felling trees and notching logs, Kerr scratched plans for a city he called Gonzales in honor of the provisional governor of Coahuila and Texas.

Then business called Kerr from the settlement. Deaf Smith and Geron Hinds went in search of buffalo, and Bazil Durbin, John and Betsy Oliver, and Kerr's black servant, Jack, set out for a Fourth of July celebration on the Colorado. On Sunday, July 2, they pitched their tents on Thorn's Branch. Around midnight, yells and gunshots aroused them from their blankets. Indians! Durbin was wounded in the shoulder but managed to join his companions in a thicket until the Redskins moved on. Eventually, the colonists made their way to Major Kerr's cabin, where they found the scalped body of John Wightman lying in a pool of blood in the dogtrot between the log sections of the house. The place had been sacked. Among items stolen were Major Kerr's field notes, sketches and three surveying compasses.[2] The settlers hurried to Berry's cabin, where they found a note scrawled in charcoal on the door, ''Gone to Burnham's on the Colorado.'' This episode left a scar that would fester for years.[3]

After the empresario's return from Missouri, guiding three new families to join the settlement, he and Kerr discussed the old site at Gonzales. Kerr argued that the location should be abandoned, that the original colonists did not have the strength to rebuild, and that a location on the Lavaca would be more desirable.[4] Prior to relocating, Kerr called upon the Mexican political chief in Bexar, asking that he assign DeWitt the entire Lavaca valley. During this trip, Kerr took careful note of the region, of which he wrote glowingly:

> No place on earth can exceed this for beauty. The Elisian fields of the Mehometan Paradise never was so delightsome as these Prairies.[5]

While the political chief did not oppose a station on the Lavaca, he did not authorize the establishment of a permanent location, and Kerr, evidently, elected to pay little attention to restrictions under the colonization laws which stated that only by special permission could the ten leagues bordering the coast be occupied by colonists. Or, perhaps Kerr believed his appearance before the chief qualified as special permission.

The colonists, assuming the government had approved, began building. Even DeWitt looked upon the Lavaca station as a place of ''shelter and safety on landing in this vast wilderness.'' Soon, approximately 40 men, women, and children called the place home. Lands had been distributed, homes were under construction, and James Norton was serving as alcalde.[6]

Colonists began their second year with seed in the ground. But this site, like the first, was doomed. Because of a quarrel between Americans and Mexicans and because authorities began to suspect that contraband trade originated at Lavaca, the location was abandoned, and some of the colonists who had left Gonzales returned; they with newcomers began constructing blockhouses in case of Indian attack.[7] With Comanche, Karankawa, Tonkawa, Waco, Tawakana, and Kechi in the area, colonists, remembering stories about the July the Fourth raid, lived in constant fear of Indian attack. In 1829, DeWitt wrote his political leader, Ramon Musquiz, requesting a detachment of troops for protection against Indians. Casually, DeWitt mentioned his belief that some contraband was passing through the territory, but he found it impossible to prevent such exchange. Apparently the cry of contraband was effective—perhaps the cry against Indians was not so loud; a detachment arrived within a few days. The troops remained but a brief time and were withdrawn. Again and again, DeWitt requested armed men to protect his settlement; again and again, the plea fell unheeded.[8]

On April 6, 1830, a law was passed that under no circumstances were foreigners to be admitted on the northern frontier of Mexico unless they were carrying passports from Mexican agents. It was interpreted that the law did not apply to DeWitt's colony, for the empresario had not yet filled his quota of settlers. Then, on Oct. 6, 1830, the vice consul of Mexico stationed in New Orleans received word that passports were to be denied all North Americans except those en route to Austin's and DeWitt's colonies.[9]

These events in Mexico—the repeated request for troops at Gonzales and the exclusion of DeWitt's colony from the list of those blacklisted for immigration—were to have far reaching effects on the 54 colonists on their way to the Gonzales settlement. Among them were the Almeron Dickinsons. Arriving with them—and evidently in the same wagon train—were Mathew Caldwell,[10] Michael Gillen, John Henry, Joseph Lawlor, John Morris, Silas M. Morris, Spencer Morris, John A. Neill, and Porter Alexander, a party of 48. Included were three single men, John E. Gavin, Joseph P. Lawlor, and John Morris. These new Texians found the soil fertile, the banks of the Guadalupe steep, and the river sometimes muddy. They perhaps were impressed with the grass, which one colonist later described as growing "abundantly upon the Guadalupe and its tributaries" and deserving "a special notice, as it is another evidence of the attention

7

of the Creator to the wants of man.'' Mesquite grass, he recorded, was ''small, delicate . . . much like the blue grass of the United States.''[11] New arrivals also noticed the spreading oaks with waxy leaves green even in February and the mesquite, stark and thorny sharp, much like the locust trees they had known at their old homes. One settler observed that they were ''too small for any use except firewood.''

No diary or journal remains telling what the Dickinsons and their traveling companions brought with them or how they made the trip from Tennessee to Texas, but if they were typical, they arrived with a minimum of equipment. And since the Dickinsons were a newly married couple, it is safe to assume that they had neither time nor money to accumulate many goods. They may have arrived in a ''Kentucky wagon'' or an old farm wagon—probably pulled by one oxen or a yoke.

The more prosperous of their associates arrived behind a mule or horse or team. Some of them brought sheep, some hogs, and some the beginning of a flock of geese or chickens. Not only were the fowls producers of eggs and the yielders of meat when their laying days were at an end, buy they also were sources of feathers or down—an essential for stuffing pillows and mattresses.[12]

Susanna, the bride, had faced the problem of preparing the larder for the Texas trip. There was a limited space for carrying provisions; often food supplies were lost along the way. What could one do when the barrel of flour resting on the wagon floor got wet in fording a stream? What could one do for cornmeal when the supply was exhausted? And how could one avoid the dullness of a routine diet? Venison and game helped, but the Dickinsons had made the trip in the autumn and winter of the year when there were no berries or fruits to offer variety. Walnuts and pecans did add some spice to several meals.

The Dickinson wagon possibly contained the barest of furniture, but it was heavy with building tools—broadaxe, hewing axe, adze, burl hammer for driving pins,[13] Dickinson, no doubt, surely had a bellows, sledge, flattening hammers, fire tongs, and hardy. And clothes? One Texian wrote:

The dress of the people varies according to the length of time they have been in Texas. Acting on my mother's advice, I brought clothes enough to last us several years; others have done the same, but the great majority brought scanty wardrobes. The question of buying dry goods here is a serious one. Calico costs seventy-five cents per yard! As money is scarce with us all, a lady seldom has more than one Texas calico dress. Men and women sometimes dress in skins.[14]

Or, the Dickinsons and the twenty families that arrived on the same date, may have made up a schooner-load. A large number of DeWitt's colonists had come on board the schooner *Dispatch*, which the empresario had engaged in the fall of 1826 for a term of four years. The schooner plied between the station on the Lavaca River in DeWitt's colony and Missouri, where most of the colonists were recruited, and touched, of course, at Memphis; thence down the Mississippi to New Orleans, where the immigrants had to secure a passport from the Mexican consul; thence along the Gulf shore to Texas. Although this arrangement expired in 1830, it probably was renewed for the remainder of DeWitt's contract with the government of Coahuila and Texas, which came to an end on April 15, 1831. But, where would the Dickinsons have boarded the schooner?

They may have ventured first to Missouri, and, once there, allowed themselves to be persuaded by one of DeWitt's agents to seek their future in Texas. Or, they may have planned on Texas from the time Susanna and Almeron first decided to locate, in which case they could have made their way overland to Memphis, or down the Hatchie River to Brownsville, Tennessee, which was only a few miles from Bolivar, where steamers came, thence to Memphis.

Almeron and Susanna Dickinson arrived in the colony on February 20, 1831, and Almeron received his title to one league of land (4,428 acres) on May 5, 1831, and possibly set out immediately in search for a suitable location. He found one on the San Marcos River, near the northern limits of the colony. He left Susanna in the care of other colonists, camped on the townsite of Gonzales—the town lots were not distributed until 1833, so housing must have been makeshift—while he scouted the banks of the Guadalupe and San Marcos rivers.[15]

Unfortunately, no documents or archives remain telling how the Dickinsons settled into the community. Nathan Boone Burkett, however, did say on one occasion, "I will say that I knew Mrs. Dickerson well, as did all the Gonzales settlers."[16]

A manuscript, "Title DeWitt's Contract," now in the General Land Office of the State of Texas, shows that the Dickinson family, consisting of two persons, arrived in the colony on Feb. 20, 1831. No doubt, upon arrival, Almeron began the series of steps that would make him a land owner. DeWitt completed a certificate showing the applicant's name, his date of arrival in the colony, the size of his family, and asked if Almeron, in the presence of the commissioner, Ramon Musquiz, had signed the required oath of allegiance.

Without difficulty, Dickinson could recall his meeting with Musquiz and his holding the quill pen as he had added his signature to the document:

> I, Almeron Dickinson, a native of the United States of the North, appear before you observing the formalities of the law, saying: that I am one of the individuals admitted by the impresario, Green DeWitt, to settle, in accordance with the state colonization law, upon lands in his colony, as will be shown by the certificate which I endorse; that I am married; and that I have not yet received the title to the land which belongs to me as a colonist. I therefore beg you that in the exercise of your functions you put me in possession of a sitio of land . . . .

This petition, along with the certificate from Green DeWitt, Dickinson presented to Musquiz. He attached an indication of the land he desired. Dickinson observed that the government required the commissioner's approval on the petition, and it was the commissioner himself who issued titles. Dickinson watched as Ramon Musquiz, on May 5, prepared the title and accompanying surveyor's field notes entitling the applicant to one sitio of land.[17]

To complete the requirement for possession of the land, Dickinson and his friends had little expense—the surveyor's fees of 8 pesos, the commissioner's fees of 15 pesos, and the price of the stamped paper upon which the original and attested copies of the title were made.[18] The colonization law provided that the sums paid to the state be set in this manner:

For a *sitio* of grazing land, thirty *pesos*; for a labor of non-irrigable land, two *pesos* and a half; and for a *labor* of irrigable land, three *pesos* and a half. These payments might be made in three installments, at the end respectively of the fourth, fifth, and sixth years.[19]

Dickinson probably observed the commissioner at work in other ways, for it was Musquiz's responsibility to supervise the laying out of new towns. For this work, he had explicit instructions:

The town was to be laid out by lines running north and south, and east and west. A square measuring one hundred and twenty varas on each side, exclusive of streets, was to be marked off and called the principal or constitutional square. The block facing this square on the east was to be set aside for a church, curate's dwelling, and other ecclesiastical buildings; that on the west was to be reserved for municipal buildings. In some suitable place, which the commissioner might choose, a square was to be laid out for a market square. The commissioner was also to select a block for a jail and a house of correction, another for buildings designed for public instruction, and another, without the limits of the town, for a cemetery. Streets were to be twenty varas wide. Town lots were to be appraised and sold at public auction, and payments made in three installments at the end respectively of six, twelve, and eighteen months. The funds obtained from the sale of lots were to go toward the building of churches in towns, and a tax of one peso was levied upon all owners of lots for the same purpose. Lots were to be given free of cost to empresarios and to all kinds of mechanics.[20]

By the time the Dickinsons arrived in Gonzales, Byrd Lockhart had surveyed the four square leagues of land. Jose

Navarro, commissioner, however, had not followed official instructions carefully, and some of the squares were not used as designated. Market square, for example, became jail square and no area was set aside for public instruction.[21]

Eventually, Dickinson saw his name on the map, indicating that lots 1 and 2 in block 16 were assigned to him Sept. 27, 1834. The clerk, however, made a spelling error and recorded the title in the name of Almeron Dickman. The deed to these lots, appraised at 8 pesos was signed by James C. Davis, president of the *ayuntamiento*. As a mechanic, Dickinson received deeds to lots 1 and 2, premium lots in block 28, deeded by James B. Patrick.[22] On Dec. 29, 1834, Dickinson received lots 2 and 3 on range 3, block 7, in outer town. Each lot was appraised at 2 pesos, and the deed was signed by J. C. Davis. The following day, Dickinson added considerably to his land holdings when Davis deeded him four lots in range 3, block 7. Each was appraised at 3.75 and was labeled in outer town west of Water Street.[23]

A settler was entitled to hold as many as four ''out'' lots and two ''in'' lots provided he improved them. Deeds to ''in'' lots and ''out'' lots were made separately, the price of each deed being 3 pesos.[24] In 1832 Lockhart had surveyed the town tract. The southwestern portion was the inner town consisting of 49 blocks, each subdivided into six lots. The remaining portion of the four league tract was outer town.[25] Dickinson paid a surveyor's fee of one peso for an ''in'' lot and two pesos for an ''out'' lot, the fee set aside to pay the surveyor's expenses and for meeting the needs of governing the community. Dickinson also paid a tax of one peso for his ''in'' lots but no tax on his ''out'' lots.[26]

A. J. Sowell, an early settler in the area, wrote that Dickinson, Baker, Tomlinson, Sowell, Montgomery and other families settled on the river above the mouth of Mill Creek. The prairie here, Sowell wrote, ''stretched away from the river without a bush to obstruct the view.'' He continued:

At times the vast herds of buffalo could be seen crossing the prairie north and coming towards the river. At times they would stampede, and the noise of their running resembled an approaching hurricane. Walnut Branch at that time was a rushing torrent fed by a large spring at its head, which sent a perfect sluice of water to the river.[27]

As Noah Smithwick recalled the area, herds of deer and antelope supplied meat for the tables, set in "rude log cabins, windowless and floorless." These houses were only "partial protection against rain and sun," but they were homes. And no doubt Susanna soon adjusted to the residence. She probably listened with pleasure to the "whippoorwill's silvery notes" and with dread to "the tuneful mosquito, whose song, like the opera singer's, has a business to it."[28]

The Dickinsons probably had milk cows, they found game in abundance, and living was cheap, so it was not surprising that Susanna eventually took a boarder. Creed Taylor,[29] after the death of his soldier father, was sent to Gonzales by his mother. He attended school and boarded with Susanna.[30] No doubt Susanna welcomed having him in the house, for there were times Almeron was called away.

The sun was setting, casting coppery red tones on the velvet green live oak leaves one day in 1832, when the peddler's wagon loaded with costly goods and accompanied by an entourage of ten Mexican horsemen, stopped at the home of John Castleman, approximately 15 miles west of Gonzales. The peddler, a Frenchman, stopped to ask about campgrounds. Castleman pointed out a large pool of water not too far from the house but insisted that the group stay near the house.

"You had better camp here by my yard. I have plenty of wood and water, and you can get all you want. The Indians are hostile. They might attack you before morning; there is no telling. You will be safe here, for my house is surrounded by strong palisades; and in case of danger, you could come inside, and I could help you to defend your property," Castleman said.

The peddler thanked him for the offer but politely rejected the hospitality. He preferred camping by the pool, he said.

Castleman bade him good night and went about securing his own property for the night.

Shortly before daybreak, Castleman was aroused from sleep by gunfire followed by yells. Dawn glowed, and he could see the Mexicans defending their poolside position. Castleman, his rifle in hand, stood at the window of his home. To join the men defending their camp was too hazardous. The Mexicans were hidden from view, but Castleman frequently saw an Indian brave jump from place to place.

By mid-morning the Mexicans had exhausted their ammunition supply, the Indians had raided the wagon, and single file, they paraded their loot by Castleman's house. He counted eighty Indians slowly walk past his window; few had firearms, but all held bows, lances, and tomahawks.

As soon as he deemed it safe, Castleman examined the battleground, mounted his horse, and headed for Gonzales to spread the news. Twenty-seven men soon were in their saddles riding toward Castleman's spread. Andrew Sowell interviewed David Darst for the story. Darst could name J. C. Darst, Dan McCoy, Mathew Caldwell, Ezekiel Williams, B. D. McClure, John Davis, Tom Malone, _____ White, Jesse McCoy, Washington Cottle, Almeron Dickinson, Dr. James H. C. Miller, A. J. Sowell, Sr., and Castleman as participants. The other names were not available.[31]

Under the leadership of McClure, the posse picked up the Indian trail through the Guadalupe Valley. The Indians had crossed Darst Creek before they began amusing themselves by unwinding spools of thread. As Sowell reported the entertainment:

They would secure the end of the thread, and then throwing the spool down, let it unwind after them as they traveled, very likely, tying it to the tails of their horses. I expect they were greatly astonished at the length of it. This thread greatly aided the settlers in trailing them. They did not seem to apprehend pursuit.[32]

Riding northwesterly, the Indians passed near the head of Mill Creek and crossed York's Creek Divide. The pursuing party camped as soon as night came. On the second night, Sowell left his bedroll to stand guard on a ridge, ''listening, and while doing so, his quick ear caught a far-off sound like Indians singing." He informed the leader, but McClure shrugged, believing the sounds were made by coyotes rather than Indians.

"Andrew, I guess you're mistaken. I cannot hear anything, and none of the scouts have heard it; let's turn in and be after them in the morning."

"All right," Sowell agreed, "but I think I heard Indians singing straight ahead of us—but a long way off."

The following morning, the Gonzales men came upon the Indian camp, two miles from where the white settlers had spent the night. The site, on a high ridge, was centered with a pole. Grass around the pole had been tramped down, indicating the Indians had danced.

"You were right, Andrew," McClure said, "We would have caught them here, had we taken your advice; but they cannot be far ahead, and we may get them yet before they reach the mountains, unless they started as early as we did. In that case, we cannot do it, as the foot of the mountains are not more than two miles off."

"They might have started three hours before day," commented one of the men. "And in that case, they are nearly to the Blanco."

The men wasted but few minutes in conjecture. Soon they had remounted and the entire troop rode toward the hills. By nightfall—still with no sight of the pursued—the whites camped in the brakes of the Blanco River. The following morning, fog blanketed their camp but failed to dampen their eagerness to begin tracking the Indians.

As the day warmed, the fog burned away. An Indian yell echoed across the river. Aware that the yell was a signal notifying other Indians of the approach of the whites, McClure ordered his troops to advance rapidly. When they entered the cedar brake on the banks of the river, McClure suggested that his men dismount, that they turn their horses loose, and that two scouts go ahead. Almeron Dickinson and James Darst agreed to serve as advance men.

As the body of the posse reached an opening, they saw the scouts returning, pursued by several Indians. McClure and others prepared to shoot but were afraid to fire for fear of endangering Dickinson and Darst. Finally, they were able to open fire. Three Indians fell, and their associates began retreating toward the river. Several more lost their lives trying to cross.

Sowell reported the results:

> The fight now being over, they began to sum up the casualties, which stood thus: None killed, some wounded and one missing. They at once commenced a search for the missing man, thinking he was killed somewhere in the brush, but their hunt was of no avail; they could not find him, and fearing their horses would wander too far off, they went to secure them before searching any more for the missing man; but while they were gathering up the horses, he came to them without hat or shoes, looking as wild as a buck . . . . He had no idea what he had done with his shoes. They were afterwards found on the bank of the river, near the edge of the water, as if he had an idea of crossing.

After collecting their horses and ''selecting as many costly goods as they could carry'' from the peddler's stock, the settlers began the return ride to Gonzales.[33]

No doubt, Susanna listened attentively as Almeron gave details of his Indian fight on the banks of the river. She had her own worries about the wild animals that lived in the Guadalupe Valley. Her apprehensions must have heightened when Andrew Sowell chased a panther into one of the trees in the neighborhood in 1833. The panther had attempted to carry off a pig, but the dogs and Andrew gave it such chase that the cat dropped the suckling and sought safety in a tree. Andrew killed the panther, but it lodged in one of the branches.

On another evening, one of the neighbors, Mrs. Isaac Baker and several dogs were walking to the Sowell place, ''built on a bluff of the Guadalupe.''[34]

A large animal suddenly confronted her; she was greatly frightened, and set the dogs on it, one of which was in-

16

stantly torn to pieces. Out of breath, nearly, she ran on to the house, and told the circumstances. The boys repaired to the spot and found the slain dog, but could not find the animal. The next day, Jim Tumlinson killed a tiger near the spot, which from her description of the animal, must have been the same.[35]

Indians gave Susanna her greatest fright. Sowell tells the story:

At one time, Indian tracks were seen in the vicinity, and shortly after, a small band of Indians made their appearance, but professed friendship. The settlers had their doubts, and kept close watch upon them. They camped about, on the river, a few days, and then disappeared, and at the same time two horses were missed from the neighborhood, and accordingly Andrew, Montgomery and three others went in quest of them. At the mouth of Mill Creek they found the missing horses in possession of two Indians. They were surrounded, and they gave them up, making no show of resistance. Their arms were taken from them, and they were escorted to the house of Dickinson, for trial, it being the nearest. Dickinson was gone and they carried the Indians in the house until they could come to some agreement as to their disposal. It was finally decided to kill them, and picking up their guns, carried them out in the yard for that purpose, but Mrs. Dickinson commenced screaming, and told them for ''goodness sake'' not to kill them in her yard. The men thought this would look a little too bad, and concluded to take them across the hollow and dispatch them in a little grove of timber on the ridge. As they walked along, Montgomery was on the right of the largest Indian. They knew their fate and commenced talking in a low tone in the Indian dialect.

Andrew, convinced that the Indians were plotting, warned Montgomery to keep an alert and to avoid walking too close to the Indian.

''All right,'' Montgomery said, ''I'm watching him. If he makes a move, I'll plug him.''

17

Almost immediately, the Indian drew a long knife "from some where about his person, and sank it in Montgomery's breast. Both Indians then broke into a run.

The settlers began firing. They downed one Indian, the one who had killed Montgomery, but in their confusion had wounded one of their own number.

The Dickinsons, like the other Gonzales settlers, were alarmed over the Indian affair; they continued to fear a general disturbance, and some of their neighbors talked of leaving Texas.[36]

As residents of Gonzales, Almeron and Susanna were under the jurisdiction of the *ayuntamiento*, whose officers were elected by the population to care for the health, comfort and safety of the people, to protect property, to preserve public peace, to manage and invest municipal funds, and to levy taxes. On Dec. 21, 1833, the *ayuntamiento* resolved that because persons appointed to appraise the "in" lots and the "out" lots of Gonzales had failed to do so, Almeron Dickinson and Green DeWitt would serve on a committee. They were asked to make a report on the evaluation of property at the next meeting of the council.

The *ayuntamiento* passed a resolution that all persons able to labor on roads and highways were "hereby bound to do so when ordered or subject themselves to pay a fine of one Dollar per day for each day they failed to do so." No individual would be required to work more than six days a year. Almeron Dickinson felt the arm of the law on Jan. 1, 1834, when he and DeWitt were appointed commissioners "to review and mark out the road from DeWitt's to intersect the old road at some suitable point crossing the river opposite of the street running by the house of Thomas R. Miller, [37] and on route to the above named point and report the same at the next meeting."

Other measures coming before the *ayuntamiento* must have interested all residents of Gonzales. Any person "who shall be found guilty of removing any stake defacing or cutting of any Corner tree or bearing tree or altering or changing land marks established by the municipal surveyor . . . shall forfeit and pay to this municipality for each offence a sum not less than one Dollar nor more than fifty Dollars.'' Another ecological measure adopted by the council was a ruling that any person shooting guns or pistols within the bounds of the ''in'' lots was subject to a fine. A fine was also levied against those individuals found guilty of running horses through the streets. And the *ayuntamiento* members saw fit to set standard charges for ferrage across the Guadalupe: 1.50 pesos for a loaded wagon and team; 1 for an empty wagon and team; 1.25 for loaded carts and teams; 75 centavos for an empty cart and team, and 75 centavos for one ''yoak of cattle.'' Individuals on business for the colony could ''pass free.''[38] The council also approved Joseph S. Martin's cutting timber off a town tract for use in erecting a cotton gin. John Francis Buchetti was hired May 28, 1833, as ''translator & Secatary and to teach a Spanish School for the term of six months,'' but on July 10, ''John Francis Buchetti . . . (was) discharged from his employment as Translator, Secatary [sic] and School-teacher.''[39]

By December, 1832, the Dickinsons had cast away all thoughts of local government, of Indian problems, of animal raids. Their concerns were of Susanna's puerperium, and on Dec. 14, their lives took on new dimension with the arrival of a daughter, Angelina Elizabeth Dickinson.

Certainly the years in Gonzales provided the opportunity to become acquainted with Ramon Musquiz, political chief who made personal inspection visits as part of his duty and sent detailed accounts of conditions as he found them in the new community. [40] Surely the Dickinsons talked about DeWitt's repeated attempts to persuade Musquiz to send for a detachment of troops for protection against Indians, and as residents of the colony they must have commented on Musquiz's communication with DeWitt that the empresario might have an unmounted cannon from Bexar if he would but send a wagon for it. On March 4, 1831, a wagon left Gonzales for the cannon, and Dickinson's interest in weapons surely demanded that he run his hands over the smooth brass barrel after the weapon's arrival in its new home. The six-pounder later would have ''an importance greater than its calibre seemed to justify.''[41] No doubt, the colonists talked about what they would do in case of an Indian raid, griped about the failure of officials to send troops for protection, and determined to fend for themselves.

Until Sept. 29, 1835, there were only 18 men in Gonzales, but they were destined to go down in Texas history as the "Old Eighteen."[42]

From the time there had been a question over the property rights, there had been a current of distrust between the Mexicans and the Americans. The Anglos, however, had decided they were more interested in peace than in pursuing cultural activities and settling legal difficulties. Then on Sept. 21, 1835, five Mexican soldiers and their corporal appeared across the Guadalupe River with demands for the cannon, the brass six-pounder that Ramon Musquiz had released to Gonzales citizens for protection against Indians.

Gonzales pioneers refused to surrender their weapon. Instead, on Sept. 29, the men of the town buried the six-pounder in George W. Davis's[43] peach orchard, plowed it under, and "smoothed over" the resting place.[44]

Two hundred Mexicans galloped to the river bank. The lieutenant in charge sent a packet of papers across to Captain Albert Martin. Inside the packet, Martin found a note from Colonel Domingo de Ugartechea, military commandant of Coahuila and Texas in charge of the forces at San Antonio de Bexar Presidio. There was a note from Ramon Musquiz. There was a piece of correspondence from Lieutenant Francisco Castañeda, in charge of seeking a conference with the military leader of the Texians. Each letter had one thing in common—demand that the brass cannon be returned.

Captain Albert Martin probably looked over his troops—18 men. Eighteen men facing a force of 200 mounted Mexicans. He must play for time, and play for time he did—replying to the correspondence with the information that the alcalde, Andrew Ponton, was away but would be back in the evening. Meanwhile, his soldiers gathered on the "prairie bluff below the town watering place just above where the timbered bottom begins."[45] Some of the families—Mrs. Dickinson and Angelina may have been among them—sought safety in the timbered bottoms.[46]

Upon receipt of the message, Lt. Castañeda ordered his troops to a piece of prairie land half a mile from the ferry, apparently biding time until he could confer with the alcalde. His delay was costly, for soon the Texians were joined by approximately 100 men from the Colorado and Brazos lands.

During the day the Mexican force made feints at the ford, half a mile below the town, and at the ferry, but learning that they would be vigorously opposed, fell back to a mound three hundred yards from the ford. Here they set up camp. To oppose them, Gonzales men set up a rude fort with a trussed top, upon which they mounted their coveted cannon. A small company under Lt. Almeron Dickinson was appointed to serve the piece.[47] These artillerymen slept by their gun; others in the Gonzales army "reposed on the bare ground."[48] Creed Taylor, a participant, told James DeShields of the respect Texians felt for the cannon:

> Of course we all felt proud of our 'artillery,' mainly for two reasons: it was the bone of contention; the Mexicans came for it and had said they were not going back without it, and by placing it in a conspicuous place in the battle line we thought it would serve to nerve them on and by that means give us a chance to humble their pride in open fight. We also cherished the idea that loaded as it was, with slugs and scrap iron, when once fired at close range it would carry slaughter into the ranks of the enemy, and those not killed outright would probably be scared off the field.[49]

David Macomb, writing of the event for the *Telegraph and Texas Register*, reported:

> Our number had increased to one hundred and sixty-eight men, and in an election for field officers, the lot fell on John H. Moore, as colonel and J. W. E. Wallace as lieutenant-colonel. About 7 o'clock on Thursday evening, our troops crossed the river; the horse to the amount of fifty, and the infantry at the ferry, together with the cannon, tolerably well mounted.''

"There was no coal, so some of the boys were set to burning charcoal. We brushed the old cannon (an iron six-pounder),[50] scoured it out, and mounted it on old wooden trucks—transverse sections of trees with holes in the centers, into which were inserted wooden axles—and christened it 'the flying artillery,' making merry over it as if it were some holiday sport we were planning for. We had no ammunition for our 'artillery,' so we cut slugs of iron bar and hammered them into balls; ugly looking missles they were I assure you, but destined to 'innocuous desuetude,' . . . ." Smithwick recalled later.[51]

Gonzales women too, did their bit—contributing their flat irons, skillets, and iron kettles. One even removed the spindle of her spinning wheel. Men donated their plows and hoes.[52]

Now "tolerably well mounted," the cannon rode a "broad-tired ox-wagon . . . fitted up."[53] The gun had been crammed with chains and scrap iron in readiness to greet the Mexicans if they crossed the Guadalupe, and one can speculate whether some of the metal may have been gathered up from Dickinson's smithy.[54]

While several Texians were manufacturing ammunition, several others were designing a flag, about which Smithwick wrote:

> I cannot say who designed it nor who executed the design, as that was not in my department, and history is silent on the subject . . . . To my certain knowledge the first Lone Star flag used in the revolution was gotten up at Gonzales for Austin's army and consisted of a breadth of white cotton cloth about six feet long, in the center of which was painted in black a picture of the old cannon, above it a lone star and beneath it the words, "Come and take it," a challenge which was lost on the Mexicans.

Lt. Col. Wallace[55] formed his command into the line of march, arranging the cavalry in advance of the cannon, with two companies of flankers, and two open columns on each side and a company of infantry in the rear. Quietly, they marched, but once they reached the point to be occupied, an advance guard took the fire of a picket guard. He was slightly injured in the nose.

Thus alerted, the Mexicans pulled themselves from their serape beds, reached for their weapons, and hurried into formation. Wallace ordered his men to form two columns, "deploying into line on the right and left—the cannon in the centre, and the cavalry occupying the extreme right." At 4 p.m. Friday, under a thick covering, the Mexicans left the position they had occupied during the night. Details of what followed were preserved by Macomb:

> Our position had been taken in the vicinity of a skirt of timber, and our troops remained under cover of it until the exact position of the Mexicans was ascertained, which did not take place until daylight. Our troops then advanced in order of battle, under cover of the fog, into the open prairie, to within about three hundred and fifty yards of the enemy. Our scouts in advance having discharged their rifles, came into the main body, having been followed nearly in by a troop of Mexicans.

Then, Col. Moore directed Lt. Dickinson and his men to open fire with the "artillery." The order was obeyed instantly, and the results were recorded by Creed Taylor:

> The shock caused by the fire of that old brass cannon seemed to jar the very earth and the sound seemed sufficient to awaken the dead. It awoke the echoes for miles around and, figuratively, it continues to reverberate around the earth as the gun that sounded the death knell of Mexican tyranny in Texas.[56]

Upon hearing the cannon fire, the Mexicans wheeled upon their horses and retreated to their old position. The Texians took over "some horses and some baggage that had been left." The fog lifted, showing the Texians in possession of Williams' plantation. Then word came that the Mexican commandant would like a meeting with Col. Moore.

Commanders of both forces—Moore and Wallace and Castañeda and one of his officers—marched to the center of the battlefield. Castañeda asked the reasons for the attack.

"You ordered the cannon, then followed with a threat, in case of a refusal, to take the weapon by force," Col. Wallace explained. "The cannon had been presented the people of Gonzales for defense of the Constitution, by the constitutional authorities. In my point of view, you as a Mexican officer are acting under orders of Gen. Santa Anna, who has broken down all state and federal constitutions. But, we will fight for our rights until the last gasp.''

''I am a republican; two-thirds of the Mexicans are such, but I'm still an officer of the federal government although that government has undergone some changes—considerable changes. The majority of the states had decided upon that change, so we, the people of Texas, are bound to submit to it. We do not want to fight you Anglo-Americans of Texas. My orders are simply to demand the cannon and if you refuse, to take up a position until further orders come,'' Castañeda explained.

Col. Moore then asked Castañeda to surrender. ''Join us and you will be received with open arms. You'll be permitted to retain your rank, pay and emoluments. Fight us and . . . .''

''I am a military man, sir. I have my orders. I am obliged to obey them.''

Exchanging courteous—if stiff—bows, the representatives of the two opposing forces returned to their commands. Almost immediately upon reaching his territory, Col. Wallace ordered troops to fire. The Texians advanced in double time. The Mexicans fled. Reason for the hasty retreat, as explained by David Macomb in his newspaper story, was:

. . . Castonado, when attacked on Friday morning, was waiting for a reinforcement, and further orders, and by the information received that night from San Antonio, Ugartechea had determined to put all his disposable force in motion, and is determined to take a sufficient number to effect his purpose. The reason assigned by Castonado for flying without giving battle, was that we had cannon, and he had none; but that when he should receive a reinforcement, Colonel Ugartechea would bring on cannon sufficient to burn and reduce the whole town to ashes.

Fully expecting another attack to follow, the journalist obviously tried to recruit for the Texians in Gonzales. He wrote:

We therefore look for another attack soon, in considerable force, and if our troops arrive soon enough, they will enable us to repel the attack successfully, and even, if thought "politic," to take up the line of march immediately for San Antonio, and two cannon mounted; about two hundred of them convicts, with ball and chain, for having attempted to desert; and at least 100 must remain to keep down the citizens, who it appears are strongly opposed to centralism. It is highly important that we should be strongly reinforced; we shall probably have, in two or three days, about from three hundred to three hundred and fifty men, and if we had about five hundred men, we could without fear of defeat, take San Antonio, Labahia, and in fact drive the entire enemy out of Texas . . . .[57]

"Well supplied with beef and bread, and corn for . . . (the) horses," the Texians began preparation for the coming battle. The grist mill, recently repaired, began turning. "We shall grind plenty of meal in advance for those that are coming. In fine, the Anglo-American spirit appears in every thing we do: quick, intelligent, and comprehensive . . . ," David P. Macomb said.

With this skirmish, the Texas Revolution had begun. While the Texians collected whatever baggage was left on the field and marched "in good order and high spirits," they failed to realize they had done little but kill one man and scare the Mexicans into retreat.[58]

They had, however, opened the floodgate to volunteers from throughout Texas—some eager for a fight, some apprehensive, some appearing because they recognized a duty. Noah Smithwick and a corps of volunteers arrived in Gonzales and immediately took charge of the cannon.

As Noah Smithwick looked back on what happened, it seemed like "egregious foolhardiness;" at the time he entered into preparations with eagerness. He remembered:

Our whole available force could not have amounted to more than 250 men, while Mexico had an organized army of several thousand, and there were thousands of Indians eagerly watching for an opportunity to swoop down on us and wipe us from the face of the earth and thus regain their lost hunting grounds . . . . That one old bushed cannon was our only artillery, and our only arms were Bowie knives and long single-barreled, muzzle-loading flintlock rifles, the same kind that our fathers won their independence with . . . ."[59]

"Burning coal, brushing cannon, repairing rifles, moulding bullets, and making flags, lances and cannon balls" left little time for the Texians to study military tactics.[60] Some busied themselves with other pursuits, however; they left Ezekiel Williams' plantation, "robbed, supplying themselves with sacks of watermelons."[61]

Texian spirits must have taken rise when Stephen F. Austin and Moses Austin Bryan arrived, for the "Father of Texas" set about unifying the troops and stimulating them in their fight for freedom. While pulling a coat closely about his shoulders and huddling closer to the campfire, Austin discussed military organization with his men. His recent imprisonment in Mexico had left Austin weak, and he coughed frequently.

Ben Milam, another who had recently escaped from a Mexican prison, joined the Texians. Milam had changed his prison rags in Goliad, accepting whatever clothing was available, and when he rode his pony into camp, the Texians must have stared at the six-footer. When he dismounted, he showed that his Mexican pantaloons were at least six inches too short, and his sleeves hit him midway between the elbow and the wrist.

When it was time to select a commander-in-chief, John A. Wharton proposed Austin. "Austin can come nearer uniting the people than any other man, and furthermore, it will give better standing abroad," he said.

Austin, despite his weakened condition and hacking cough, agreed to serve the Texians. The new commander must have been encouraged by the number of recruits daily joining his forces, but he was concerned over their equipment and clothing. Many wore buckskin breeches—some black and shiny and hard but some new and soft and yellow; some had "assumed an advanced position at the knee, followed by a corresponding shortening of the lower front length, exposing shins as guiltless of socks as a—Kansas Senator's.'' Some of the soldiers walked in boots; some moccasins. Some wore broad-brimmed hats; some coonskin caps with the tails hanging down the back. Some rode big American horses; some straddled small methodical mules. For canteens, each carried a Spanish gourd, and his frying pan dangled from his pack. ''Here a bulky roll of red quilts jostled a pair of 'store' blankets; there the shaggy brown buffalo robe contrasted with a gaily checkered counterpane on which the manufacturer had lavished all the skill of dye and weave known to the art—mayhap it was part of the dowery a wife brought her husband on her wedding day, and surely the daydreams she wove into its ample folds held in them no shadow of a presentiment that it might be his winding sheet.[62]

On Oct. 13, the men broke camp—their destination, San Antonio. The ''flying artillery'' was pulled by two yokes of long-horned Texas steers. Over it flew the ''old cannon flag,'' and behind, men—approximately 600 of them—filed. Sometimes they prodded the oxen, and when the animals broke into a trot, the cannon bumped and screeched. The force was now 500-600, following the cannon flag, ''proudly borne by a man mounted upon a small wiry pony that had an inclination to dash off at full speed every time the boys gave vent to their feelings with a ringing cheer.''[63] Immediately behind the color guard were the artillery, commanded by Lt. Almeron Dickinson.

Toward evening that first day of march, the gun carriage broke while crossing a creek, was tugged to dry land and repaired. The column of infantry marched on. Creed Taylor told James T. DeShields his attitude at the time:

. . . from that hour the old cannon was in the rear and by its occasional breaking down became the source of more delay and vexation than any other feature of the march. We managed to patch up the frail running gear until we reached Sandy Creek and went into camp, when Captain Dickenson [sic] informed the general that in order to proceed further with a gun, a more substantial carriage would have to be provided.

Before camp broke the following morning, a number of Texians visited "artillery headquarters" to view the wrecked artillery piece. Several leaders suggested repairing the piece; some recommended abandoning it. Some argued that unless a supply of ammunition were brought from Goliad, the cannon would be useless. Taylor told DeShields:

> . . . The gun was abandoned, the army took up the line of march, and I never saw the old piece again. I was told, and it was common report among the boys in the ranks, that Captain Dickenson [sic] had the gun buried on the spot; and in order to conceal its resting place from enemy scouts who might chance that way, the ruins of the truck, with wood and brush, was piled upon the shallow grave and burned . . . ."[64]

At Cibolo, some 25 miles from San Antonio, Sam Houston rode into camp, "mounted on a little yellow Spanish stallion so diminutive that old Sam's legs, incased in the conventional buckskin almost touched the ground."[65] After saluting Austin, Houston trotted his mount to the front of the marching soldiers so he could inspect them as they straggled by. While Houston inspected the troops, a flock flew overhead; several shots rang out. Aware that Austin had instructed his men to conserve ammunition, Houston became alert to the lack of discipline. He recognized the poor equipment. And that night, when he talked with Austin, Houston could not refrain from mentioning these problems.

Austin, drawing his coat tighter around his thin body, listened. Between coughing attacks, he explained how he had organized the troops and how he had awarded several commissions. The exact number and the names of the officers he was not certain of at this time. He had, he remembered, named Lt. Almeron Dickinson, the blacksmith of Gonzales, in charge of artillery. He had given some kind of rank to James Bowie who had galloped into camp on a small gray mare with six volunteers from Louisiana. Houston may have noticed Bowie—he had a knife in his sash and his rifle was slung over his shoulder.[66] And he may have given a commission to Milam, the man wearing the shrunken Mexican pantaloons.

Houston discussed his reason for visiting camp. Could Austin persuade the delegates to return to the Consultation so that the Texas government could be organized?

The following morning, Austin spoke to his troops, and they agreed that the delegates had a duty to form a government. Still fighting chills and coughs, Austin told the Texians, "Retreat is now impossible; we must go forward to victory or die the death of traitors."

"I will wear myself out by inches rather than submit to Santa Anna's arbitrary," Austin said, feeling a chill although the day was warm.

Although little is known about the activities of Susanna Dickinson at the time, letters L. Smither addressed to "Jeneral Steven F Austen at Head quartr" give some information. Smither began his first letter to Austin on Nov. 4, 1835, and headed the message "Gonzelas." He wrote:

> Dear Sir you have placed me at this place to attind to such matters as directed with all sober and honest men in this place knows that I have attended to them day and night the companes that is coming on when in this place has broken open allmost Evry house in this place and stole 100 dollars or thir about of Miller and Treated the wimon of this place worse than all the comanshee nation could have done and draged me out of the house and nearly beat me to death becos I was in the house of Mr. Dickerson ho thiy I have no doubt the would have kild if I had not bean there there is no authority nor people to punish such people and if the army dosnot protect the people at this plac it must bee Intirely abanded by the Inhabtants . . . .[67]

A second letter also addressed Nov. 4, 1835, went from Smither to Stephen F. Austin telling more details about problems in Gonzales:

> Dear Sir I Regret to bee compeld to address you on such a savage and hostile Conduct as was commitd by some of the troops that past this place on yesterday or rather come into the place on yesterday after beeing guilty of all the bad con-

duct and Language that Sivelize beeing could put up with, after Night there ware a mass Rased among them with a young Mr. thompson at the head of them ho can bee degnated by nombers of the men and broke open all most Every house in town and Robed all they could Lay ther hands on and such Insults wire never offerd to american women before thire is no tribe of savages of Mexicans that would be guilty of such conduct after working on the boat until 9 or 10 o'clock and finding the mob in town Mrs. Dickerson ho had been drivin from her house cald on me to go and stay in her house to protect her person and property

after goind to Bead thiy Enterd the house twice by bursting Evry door and window and coming in crowds and dragd me into the Streats and beat my head to a poltice and sould have kild me in the most torturing manner for no caws on earth but that I was in the house I used Evey means to pasefy them but the wild savage would have adherd with more humility I Refur you to Evry sober and honable man in this place what my conduct has bean as Regards using Every means day and night to ade and assist Evry man that has past this place and If the authority of this army dos not take some steps to stop such conduct the wild savages would be preferable to the Insults of such Canebols . . . .[68]

With Houston heading east to San Felipe, Austin and his 600 Texians began marching toward San Antonio. At the San Antonio River, near the old San Jose Mission, troops halted. Col. Bowie with the companies of James Fannin and Coleman reconnoitered before selecting a position from which to direct operations against the San Antonio garrison. Their only opposition was from a party of Mexican soldiers ''who came up and fired on us at long range.'' The Texians returned the fire, and the Mexicans fled.

We went on up, made our observations, and camped in a bend of the river on the east side, about a quarter of a mile above the old mission of Concepcion and distant some two miles from San Antonio, expecting the main army to follow right on, but for some reason Colonel Austin did not do so. Just about sundown we were startled by a dull boom and, ere we had time to frame a question as to its import, a cannon ball, shot from a gun mounted in the church tower two miles away, shrieked through the air overhead and buried itself in the earth a few rods beyond our camp. With a horrible hiss that no language can describe, another and another followed, to the number of a half a dozen; then, all was still. At dawn we were roused by the discharge of musketry, and directly our pickets came running in. One man had his powder horn shot away. Another fell as soon as we got into camp, and we thought he was killed; but on examination, found that his only injury consisted in a sick stomach caused by a bullet striking and breaking a large Bowie knife which he carried stuck around the waistband of his pantaloons directly in front. The knife saved his life, but he was incapacitated from taking part in the fight.[69]

The heavy fog—pewter colored—lifted showing that the enemy had crossed the river, low at this time—moved up an open plain. The Texians reined their horses out of range and sought protection under the bank of the river. Fannin's company occupied the lower arm; Coleman's the upper. And as the fog continued to clear, the Texians saw that they were surrounded except at the rear where they were protected by timber and the bluff. When the Mexicans opened fire with cannon, the Texians, lying low, watched the grape and canister crash into the pecan trees at their rear.

"Keep under cover, boys, and reserve your fire; we haven't a man to spare," Bowie called. When he saw the Mexicans move within range of Fannin's men, he ordered Coleman to support Fannin. What happened then, Smithwick recalls:

Our long rifles—and I thought I never heard files crack so keen, after the dull roar of the cannon—mowed down the Mexicans at a rate that might well have made braver hearts than those encased in their shriveled little bodies recoil. Three times they charged, but there was a platoon ready to receive them. Three times we picked off their gunners, the last one with a lighted match in his hand; then a panic seized them, and they broke. They jumped on the mules attached to the caisson, two or three on a mule, without even taking time to cut them loose, and struck out for the fort, leaving the loaded gun on the field. With a ringing cheer we mounted the bank and gave chase. We turned their cannon on them . . . .[70]

Flushed with the easy victory over the Mexicans at the battle of Concepcion, the Texians were ready to make an assault on Bexar.

General Austin, however, announced to the Consultation his desire to be relieved of his command, declaring that his "worn out constitution is not adapted to a military command." His resignation was accepted, and on November 14, 1835, Sam Houston accepted the leadership.[71]

CHAPTER THREE

SAN ANTONIO YEARS

POSSIBLY because the men in both families were Masons, Ramon and Francisca de Casteñada Musquiz welcomed Susanna and Almeron Dickinson and their 15 month-old daughter into their home in San Antonio. Musquiz probably had become well acquainted with Almeron from visits to Gonzales, and each was aware that the other was a brother Mason.[1] As political chief of Bexar, Ramon had visited the community to see that the laws of the colony were being observed, and it was he who had called for assigning troops to DeWitt's colony to avoid contraband traffic and to prevent Indian raids. Although he now was governor of Coahuila and Texas, he had remained a hospitable man. "*Mi casa es su casa*," he and his wife had said convincingly and repeatedly in welcoming the Texian couple and their child.[2]

The Musquiz stone *casa*, located on the southwest corner of Portero Street and Main Plaza, became home for the Dickinsons. Here, in their own quarters, the Dickinsons welcomed Davy Crockett and the Pennsylvanian David Cummings as boarders.[3] And here, on January 18, 1836, Dr. John Sutherland,[4] found a place to take meals. Dr. Sutherland wrote:

On reaching the old Mexican town, I sought private quarters and was fortunate in securing lodging with Lt. Almeron Dickenson and wife who were keeping house there. Here I became acquainted with all the Texans of the place, of whom there were some one hundred and fifty, these being a part of the force that had captured the place from General Cos the month previous.[5]

Although Sutherland neglected to mention the type of fare Susanna served the boarders, he did comment that the troops, the Texians in San Antonio "had with them almost everything in the way of supplies, and more than their share of the scant supply of clothing, blankets, and medicine." Yet, beef and corn, he learned later, were becoming scarce.[6]

When she was not planning and preparing meals for her boarders, Susanna did the laundry, taking her own family's wash and David Cummings's rough homespun to the San Antonio River, later spreading the clothing on the willow branches to dry and bleach in the sun. While Susanna prepared meals and did the laundry, Almeron worked on the Alamo's artillery, and by the middle of February, he had wrestled all but three guns into position.

At noon one day the bell in the squat, stone belfry of San Fernando clanged.

"The enemy . . . in view," the watchman called as he tugged the rope attached to the bell. He pointed to the west.

Hearing Texians faced the west, seeing only the plains, silver in the mid-day sun.

"False alarm," they shrugged.

Two Texians, however, agreed to ride to a rise outside town to scan the countryside. They had been gone but a short time when they began racing back, and the San Fernando bell resumed its clanging.

The Mexicans were coming into San Antonio.

While most of the Texians were scurrying into the Alamo on Feb. 23, Dickinson galloped to attend his family at the Musquiz residence. Without dismounting, he called to Susanna from the doorway. ''Give me the baby; jump up behind me, and ask no questions.''

Susanna asked no questions. Holding her child in one arm, she mounted behind her husband, and they turned their backs on the house. Dickinson spurred his horse through the water at the ford;[7] they felt the spray of water as bullets pinged into the river. On through LaVilla and down the street toward the Alamo, Dickinson urged his mount. What the Dickinsons saw must have been similar to the scene described by Alamo authority Reuben Potter:

> Bowie with a detachment was engaged in breaking open deserted houses in the neighborhood and gathering corn, while another squad was driving cattle into the in-closure east of the long barrack. Some of the volunteers, who had sold their rifles to obtain the means of dissipation, were clamoring for guns of any kind; and the rest, though in arms, appeared to be mostly without orders or a capacity for obedience. No ''army in Flanders'' ever swore harder. But one officer seemed to be at his proper post and perfectly col-lected. This was an Irish captain named Ward,[8] who, though generally drunk was now sober, and stood quietly by the guns of the south battery ready to use. Yet, amid the disorder of that hour no one seemed to think of flight.[9]

No one, except Nat Lewis,[10] merchant, who hastened from the scene. Children, playing on Main Plaza, watched Santa Anna's personal staff arrive in front of San Fernando Church. Enrique Esparza, 12, one of the group, recalled the scene:

> I saw him dismount. He did not hitch the horse. He gave the bridle to a lackey. He and his staff proceeded immediate-ly in the house on the northwest corner of Main Plaza. I will never forget the face or the figure of Santa Anna. He had a very broad face and high cheek bones. He had a hard and cruel look and his countenance was a very sinister one.[11]

When some of his playmates ran to tell their fathers in the Alamo of the arrival of El Presidente, Enrique accompanied them. He continued his account:

It was twilight when we got into the Alamo and it grew pitch dark soon. All of the doors were closed and barred. The sentinels that had been on duty without were first called inside and then the openings closed. Some sentinels were posted upon the roof, but these were protected by the walls of the Alamo church, and the old convent building (the Long Barrack.) We went into the church portion. It was shut up when we arrived. We were admitted through a small window.

I distinctly remember that I climbed through the window and over a cannon that was placed inside the church immediately behind the window. There were several other cannon there. The window was opened to permit us to enter, and it was closed immediately after we got inside.

We had not been in there long when a messenger came from Santa Anna calling for us to surrender. I remember the reply to this summons was a shot from one of the cannon on the roof of the Alamo. Soon after it was fired, I heard Santa Anna's cannon reply. I heard his cannon shot strike the walls of the church and also the convent. Then I heard the cheers from the Alamo gunners and the deriding jeers of Santa Anna's troops.[12]

In 1718 Mission San Antonio de Valero was begun—a small rock, adobe, wood, and clay mortar mission approximately 225 square feet. The mission stood only a few years, crumbling when winds from a Gulf of Mexico hurricane swept inland. Patiently the padres rebuilt, some legends insisting that they mixed the mortar with asses' milk and others suggesting that eggs from wild birds provided adhesion. Limestone came from the quarries along the San Antonio River. This mission soon collapsed, and again Franciscan friars began building[13] the largest and best fortified mission in Texas. Around its walls were holes through which muskets could be fired; over the gate a turret supported three cannon. A well, on grounds behind the chapel, promised a good supply of water. But, the church was never completed. The project, however, is described by James Wakefield Burke:

The chapel supported two towers flanking a carved doorway. The baptistry and chapel was located at the front, the nave proceeding five bays to a crossing where, past a transept projected out on either side, one entered the sanctuary. The plan was almost identical to that of the preserved Mission La Purisima Conception. An early description of the sanctuary gives this picture: ". . . A well furnished room with drawers and closets in which the ornaments were kept. There were three chalices with their patens, four cruets, a mounted crucifix, a censer, and three anointers, all of silver. For the celebration of the Holy Sacrifice and other liturgical functions there were fourteen complete sets of vestments, some of Persian silk and some of damask, besides four copes. There were also twenty chalices and fifteen sets of altar cloths. The mission had three missals, two rituals, and all the things necessary for adequate celebration of the various festivals.''

On the right hand side of the church (extending to the far side of what today is Houston Street) stretched the walled patio bordered by buildings with two-storied arched galleries. In these were offices and rooms for workshops and storage of materials. There was a large hall where there were four looms. Here cotton and woolen cloth and blankets of various kinds were woven to supply all the needs of the mission. Adjoining the looms were two rooms in which were kept the wool, the cotton, the combs, cards, spools, and other spinning accessories used by the Indians in the daily tasks. Both the wool and cotton used were raised by the mission. On the ground floor were the shops for heavier manufacture, such as the iron works, the blacksmith shop, brick and tile making.

The quarters for the neophytes consisted of buildings arranged in a square of several tiers, through the center of which ran a waterway shaded by willows and some fruit trees. All houses were provided with doors and windows and each one had bunk-type beds and chests of drawers. Each family had its pots and pans and all necessary utensils, supplied from the common warehouse. In the granary,

37

which was a large stone building, the supplies were kept. Here there was room for as many as eighteen hundred bushels of corn and several hundred bushels of beans, which were the annual harvest raised by the mission Indians. For the cultivation of their crops, chiefly corn, beans, chili, cotton, and some vegetables, the mission had forty yokes of oxen fully equipped, thirty plows and the necessary plowshares and harrows; twelve carts to transport supplies, stone and timber; fifty axes, forty hoes, twenty-two bars and twenty-five scythes. For carpentry they had all the necessary instruments and tools, such as planes, saws, vices, hammers, files, chisels, and braces. They also had a well-equipped blacksmith shop to repair their tools, sharpen their instruments, and shoe their stock.

Beyond the mission irrigation ditches had been constructed, fields were planted, and orchards flourished. The mission also had extensive ranch lands, which grazed large herds of cattle, horses, mares, mules, and goats and sheep. Mission San Antonio de Valero, at the height of its prosperity, was one of the most prosperous of the Spanish missions.''[14]

By 1790, the mission was declining, its lands and animals already divided among the neophytes, and three years later, the archives were removed to San Fernando Church. During the war for Mexican Independence from Spain, a company of Spanish soldiers from Alamo del Parras, Coahuila, Mexico, was quartered in the mission and may have been responsible for the name Alamo's being attached to the buildings. Or, Alamo, the Spanish word for cottonwood, may have come from the grove of trees along the *acequia*. The site was occupied by Mexican soldiers under General Martin Perfecto de Cos until December, 1835, when the fortress was surrendered to Texians.

On Feb. 23, 1836, a small band of Texians under Col. William Barret Travis entered the Alamo.[15]

Travis glanced up from the letter he had finished scrawling to David Ayers, in whose home near Washington-on-the-Brazos his son was living while he attended school. Travis paid little attention to Angelina Dickinson playing on the floor at his feet; instead, he scanned the note once more:

> Take care of my little boy. If the country should be saved, I may make him a splendid fortune; but if the country should be lost and I should perish, he will have nothing but the proud recollection that is the son of a man who died for his country.

He ran his hand through his red hair, then he dropped the letter into the packet for which a messenger was waiting. As the courier left the Alamo, Travis called to him to remind any recruits coming in to the Alamo to bring rations for at least ten days.[16]

The tall Alabaman then may have spent several moments in reverie—reviewing the full life he had packed into his 26 years, and he must have questioned what he was doing in Texas. He had been admitted to the bar and had served as adjutant of the 26th Regiment, Eighth Brigade, Fourth Division of the Alabama militia. He could remember some rewarding times at gaming tables. Unrewarding times, too, like the occasion he left a flannel shirt, drawers, and handkerchief as security for a gambling debt, or when he lost a suit and $14.[17]

But there had been better times. Times when he selected with care the ointment with which he dressed his hair, when he dashed bergamot or lavender lotion on his face before going to a ball—wearing hose and soft pumps, not the type of boots which now encased his tired feet.[18]

Then there had been the affair of his wife—the story that she had been involved with a riverboat gambler. There had been the trial in which Travis was charged with murder. Then it was that he had stolen to Texas. There was the daughter, Susan Isabella, born three months after he had left his old home. Perhaps it was the thought of this daughter he had never seen that caused him to pull from his finger the hammered gold ring set with black cat's eye. He slipped it on a string, knotted it, and draped the necklace around the neck of Angelina Dickinson still playing at his feet.[19] No doubt as he hugged the child, Travis thought of the person who had presented the ring to him. Rebecca Cummings.[20] On March 13, 1834, in return for a breast pin, she had slipped the hoop of gold on his finger, and he had begged for a lock of her hair.[21]

The ring,[22] Travis thought, would be one bright object to amuse the dark-haired child during the long hours of battle that loomed ahead like a dark purple cloud.

While his daughter played at Travis' feet, Almeron Dickinson and his men worked on their guns. Dr. Amos Pollard[23] inventoried medical supplies. Twenty-nine-year-old Sam Blair cut up horseshoes his troops would cram down the barrels of their cannon, and from the courtyard came the sound of barked commands as H. J. Williamson, unable to forget his days at West Point, drilled the Texians.[24]

Davy Crockett, going from one coterie of soldiers to another, spun yarns in a Tennessee brogue and played on his fiddle. A tall individual with dark complexion, Crockett wore a long buckskin coat and on his head was "a round cap without any bill, made out of fox skin with the long tail hanging down his back."[25]

Also in the Alamo was James Bowie—a handsome man of six feet, 190-pounds. He had been an expert alligator wrestler, a slave dealer; he had looked for the lost San Saba silver mines; he had won the love of the beautiful Ursula Veramendi, daughter of the lieutenant governor of Coahuila-Texas. But, now all seemed lost. Ursula and his two children had died of cholera.[26] Fever burned his own body, he was unable to lift his head from the pillow, and he fell into spasms of coughing "every few minutes." Crockett, tossing his head so that the tail of his fur cap fell down his back, sat on the floor by Bowie's cot in the room "he had occupied from the beginning of the siege."[27]

"They'll soon destroy every barricade at that front door," Bowie said, then began another coughing fit."

"And with this arsenal," Crockett said, grinning, "you could stop a whole regiment. A whole regiment."

Long lines of Mexican infantry followed by dragoons were filing into the plaza.

"All right," Crockett said. "Boys," he added volume to his voice. "Boys, aim well." The words whistled through his lips, mingling with the storm of fire that pelted the walls. The earth seemed to tremble as the Mexican assault opened.

What happened then was later reported by Susanna Dickinson in this manner:

. . . As the victorious Mexicans entered the room, he (Bowie) killed two of them with his pistols before they pierced him with their sabers."[28]

Joe added the details that "he was shot several times through the head, his brains spattering upon the wall near his bedside."[29] Dr. Sutherland, visiting the Alamo two years after the conflict, found the "marks of Bowie's brains still visible on the wall." They remained so until the wall was plastered over.[30]

Galba Fuqua stole into the room where Susanna watched Angelina, and Susanna looked at the 16-year-old. Only days earlier he had been so enthusiastic about his venture into the adult world. Pale now—his enthusiasm drowned by the constant noise—Galba tried to talk. Susanna could understand nothing he said. His jaws had been shattered, blood seeped from the angry flesh.

Again the stripling tried to talk, bracing his jaws with his hands. But, it was futile, and the youth merely nodded his head and fled from the room.[31]

What was he trying to say? Would she ever be able to remove the sight from her mind? Susanna might have dwelled on the pitiful youth if it had not been for the cannon fire and the rivers of Mexicans that swept against the rock fortress wall.

Lt. Dickinson's men continued to man the 12-pounders, but the church began to give way—the timbers holding the platform, the thick walls, the heavy wooden doors.

After the struggle had continued for hours, Dickinson rushed into the church. "Great God, Sue! The Mexicans are inside our walls! All is lost! If they spare you, love our child!'' Dickinson kissed Susanna, then drew his sword and returned to duty.

Three unarmed Texians later came to the room but were shot.

Jacob Walker, who only days earlier had talked about his children in Nacogdoches, broke into the room where Susanna awaited. Four Mexican soldiers soon entered the room. Susanna fell to her knees in prayer, but she heard a shot, and she saw the Mexicans raise Walker's body with their bayonets, as if he were a ''bundle of fodder.''[32]

The Mexicans herded the women and children of the Alamo into a corner. For a quarter of an hour, fire continued to rake the building—even after the Texians were stilled. As unsettling as the cannon fire had been, silence—heavy, stifling, sickening settled over the fortress, and Susanna crouched against the cold, musty wall, her baby warmed against her breast. A guard stood over Susanna and the other women and their children. Then, at daylight some of the women were marched away.[33]

''Is Mrs. Dickinson here?'' someone asked some time later.

Stunned into consciousness, Susanna was pulling her thoughts together when she again heard the words in broken English. ''Is Mrs. Dickinson here? If you value your life, speak up. It's a matter of life and death.''

Susanna stumbled to her feet and the center of the room, facing Gen. Manuel F. Castrillon. Some authorities insist that Susanna, following the instructions her husband had given her during their last moments together, displayed Dickinson's white sheepskin Masonic apron. Nevertheless, one of the Mexican soldiers accompanying Castrillon moved to grab Susanna's arm, but the leader rebuffed him. ''Let her alone. The general has need of her.'' When the soldier released the woman's arm, she fell in line behind the Mexicans. As they walked from the church, Susanna heard the whirring of a bullet and felt a sting in the calf of her right leg. She had been shot—intentionally or accidentally, she would never learn.[34] The pain in her calf came about the same time she felt the agony over recognizing the still body of Davy Crockett—between the church and the long barrack. Crockett's hat was close by. Only a short time earlier, Crockett had come to her apartment, fallen on his knees, "committed himself to God."[35]

When Susanna was helped into Santa Anna's quarters,[36] she could smell the coffee El Presidente had ordered his black servant, Ben, to keep on flames throughout the conflict. No doubt, while someone dressed the wound, she sipped a cup of the brew. Santa Anna pleaded with Susanna to let him send her to Mexico City, where Angelina could live as his own child. Susanna looked at her baby, playing on the dictator's lap as contentedly as she had once patted her own father's face, and later had, in her childish way, wooed Travis. In Mexico, the dictator insisted, Angelina could be brought up properly. She would attend the best schools. She would want for nothing. She would wear the finest clothes. Susanna protested adamantly.[37]

Aware that he could not convince the dark-haired beauty, Santa Anna called for Ben, who had stoked up the fire under the coffee. Clumsily, Ben crossed the room. Ben would, Santa Anna declared in a tone marked with disgust, accompany Mrs. Dickinson and her child and would act as a courier, delivering a message to the Texian General, Houston.[38] To deaden the mental and physical anguish, Mrs. Dickinson asked for a second cup of coffee and sipped it while the Mexican general set about composing a letter.

Dating his letter Bexar, March 7, 1836, the day after the Alamo fell, Santa Anna wrote:

> The General-in-Chief of the Army of Operations of the Mexican Republic, to the inhabitants of Texas: Citizens! The causes which have conducted to this frontier a part of the Mexican Army are not unknown to you, a parcel of audacious adventurers, maliciously protected by some inhabitants of a neighboring republic dared to invade our territory, with the intention of dividing amongst themselves the fertile lands that are contained in the spacious Depart-

ment of Texas; and even had the boldness to entertain the idea of reaching the capital of the republic.

It became necessary to check and chastise such enormous daring; and in consequence, some exemplary punishments have already taken place in San Patricio, Lipantitlan and this city.

I am pained to find amongst those adventurers the names of some colonists, to whom had been granted repeated benefits, and who had no motive of complaint against the government of their adopted country.

These ungrateful men must also necessarily suffer the just punishment that the laws and the public vengeance demand. But if we are bound to punish the criminal, we are not the less compelled to protect the innocent. It is thus that the inhabitants of this country, let their origin be what it may, who should not appear to have been implicated in such iniquitous rebellion, shall be respected in their persons and property, provided they come forward and report themselves to the commander of the troops within eight days after they should have arrived in their respective settlements, in order to justify their conduct and to receive a document guaranteeing to them the right of enjoying that which lawfully belongs to them.

Bexarians! Return to your homes and dedicate yourselves to your domestic duties. Your city and the fortress of the Alamo are already in possession of the Mexican Army, composed of your own fellow citizens; and rest assured that no mass of foreigners will ever interrupt your repose, and much less, attack your lives and plunder your property. The Supreme Government has taken you under its protection and will seek for your good.

Inhabitants of Texas! I have related to you the orders that the army of operation I have the honor to command comes to execute; and therefore, the good will have nothing to fear. Fulfill always your duties as Mexican citizens, and you may expect the protection and benefit of the laws; and rest assured that you will never have reason to repent yourselves of having observed such conduct, for I pledge you in the name of the supreme authorities of the nation, and as your fellow citizen and friend, that what has been promised you will be faithfully performed.

Antonio Lopes de Santa Anna.[39]

Meanwhile, through chilly, wet weather, over muddy roads, through swollen streams, Sam Houston and his Texians marched. Troops ran into Texians abandoning their homes. No one on the road could give information about the Alamo, but Houston feared the rumors he and his Texians had heard were true. On March 11, Houston and his Texians joined the camp of volunteers at Gonzales, 76 miles from San Antonio.

Darkness had not settled on the camp when two Mexicans, claiming to be friendly, rode into camp with news that the mission fortress had fallen. They reported that Santa Anna had begun attacking at 3 p.m. Sunday, and five hours later, the fight was over; remains of the defenders were being burned in the public square. One of the Mexicans, Anselmo Borgara, told Houston, and the general mentioned it in a letter to Col. Fannin at Goliad:

After the fort was carried seven men surrendered, and called for Santa Anna and quarter. They were murdered by his order, Colonel Bowie was sick in bed, and also murdered .... The bodies of Americans were burnt after the massacre .... Lieutenant Dickinson, who had a wife and child in the fort, after having fought with desperate courage, tied his child to his back and leaped from the top of a two-story building. Both were killed by the fall.[40]

After repeating the story, Houston added:

I have little doubt but that the Alamo has fallen— whether above particulars are all true may be questionable.[41]

Houston ordered the messengers held under arrest so that he could question them, and while he did so, 20 men in camp left, saying they had to look after their families.[42] Taking time from the inquiry, Houston ordered two extraordinary men to ride toward San Antonio to learn the true situation. For scouts, he selected Henry Karnes, 24, whose boyhood in Arkansas had given him training in hunting and trapping. Erastus "Deaf" Smith, 49, had married a Mexican widow; he knew Mexican customs and language, and his loss of hearing as a child had sharpened his other senses. Houston poured out instructions. Learn what had happened at the Alamo. Find out what Santa Anna's plans were. Would they serve as scouts? Did they need other men to ride with them?

Young Karnes left the answering to the stocky Smith, whose high squeaky voice uttered a "yes" and a "no"—a "yes" to serving, a "no" to needing assistance.

John and Sarah Nash Bruno[43] were in their home three miles from Gonzales. About 9 o'clock a disturbance pulled John to the door.

"Hello, the house," called a woman from horseback. She cradled a child in her arms.

Immediately John and Sarah rushed into the yard, and Susanna Dickinson handed the woman Angelina. John helped Susanna dismount, then began leading the horse to the stable. While he removed the saddle, Sarah and Susanna took Angelina into the house. Sarah immediately began preparing a supper of cornbread, salt pork, and beef. When John was back in the house, Susanna began talking, describing for the first time the final hours of the Alamo siege.

She told of how she and the baby had stayed in the powder magazine all night and morning preceding the fall, of how when no one was left alive in the room the Mexican commander had told all who were alive to speak up if they would save their lives. Mrs. Dickinson then spoke up—and immediately was taken by a Mexican to Santa Anna.[44]

Susanna, Angelina sharing the saddle with her, and Ben, carrying the message from Santa Anna to the inhabitants of Texas, rode from San Antonio. Slowly, they traveled over the road eastward. They had gone several miles beyond the Salado when a rustling in the tall grass shied the horses. A robust black, flushed from the bushes, Susanna recognized as Joe, the 23-year-old slave who had served Travis. Capt. William F. Gray, after hearing Joe tell what happened at the Alamo, said he did so with ''much modesty, apparent candor and remarkably distinctly for one of his class.''[45] When she questioned him, Joe told how he had been pulled from his hiding place in the Alamo and taken before the Mexican leader. Santa Anna had told him ''his master had behaved like a brave man,'' and since he was not waging war on Negroes, if Joe wanted his freedom it was his. Joe recognized an opportunity when he saw one.[46]

Susanna perhaps welcomed Joe as another reason for traveling slowly; Joe tagged behind them. Ben riding alongside the widow told her how he had served as a steward on a ship before becoming Juan Almonte's servant and how he had waited on his master and Santa Anna the past several days.[47]

Susanna continued her story, how Santa Anna had ordered three soldiers to guard her beyond the third picket line, and how she had been told ''to proceed along that same beef trail until she came to the first lighted house.'' She had done so; here she was.

At first, Joe and Ben remained hidden in the underbrush near the house, but the following day she coaxed them to eat and they prepared to travel on toward Gonzales.[48] One source insists that Susanna remained with the Bruno family until word came that Sam Houston had called for the evacuation of the outpost at Goliad and had insisted that all Texians flee beyond the Trinity for protection. The Bruno family, including Martha Ann, two years old, and Mrs. Dickinson and Angelina, were loaded in an ox cart heading for Mrs. Bruno's old home on Nash Creek.[49]

Some sources insist that near the Cibolo Creek, halfway between San Antonio and Gonzales, Susanna met Col. James Clinton Neill, returning from his furlough to assume command of the Alamo. Taking Angelina in his arms, Col. Neill wheeled his mount and rode with the party in search of Sam Houston.[50]

Approximately 20 miles from Gonzales, Susanna and her associates were alerted to the sound of horses. Who was in the party? Was Col. Neill?[51]

Joe urged Susanna to hide in the grass. "Might be Comanches," he warned.

"This is a bold prairie, and if it is an enemy, we must meet them face to face," Susanna said.

As the riders drew closer and Joe could see the martingales, he bounced with joy. "They're white men, Mrs. Dickinson," he declared.[52]

When the riders drew up, Susanna identified herself as the widow of Capt. Almeron Dickinson who had perished in the Alamo. Then she began to tell what had happened to the band of defenders.[53]

After listening to Susanna sob out the story of what had happened in the Alamo, stocky Karnes, his bright red hair glistening in the Texas sun, in his usual modest manner, volunteered to rush the news to Gen. Houston. Erastus Smith would accompany the Alamo survivors at a more deliberate speed.[54]

As soon as Karnes pointed his mount toward Gonzales, Erastus took Angelina in his arms, no doubt thinking of his own four children, ranging in ages from 8 to 13. Surely, as Deaf Smith galloped alongside Susanna, he fired one question after another about individuals he had known who had given their lives in the mission. Smith, 49, already had lines forming around his pecan-colored eyes, his reddish hair was tousled, and his beard grizzled, yet he treated Angelina with tenderness, and the child nestled against his dingy buckskin clothes.[55]

As they rode, Susanna and Smith talked about Gonzales.

What about Johnny Gaston? Johnnie Kellog? And old man Thomas Miller?

All dead, Susanna answered solemnly.

"Poor Sidney," Smith remarked. Then he and Susanna discussed the strange chain of events that had taken the three men to the Alamo. Johnny Gaston was but 16, and from a perch in a live oak tree he had watched the men fire the Gonzales cannon that opened this entire campaign. Some of the Gonzales folk called him Johnny Davis because his mother had married a second time; this wedding to a man named Davis mattered little to Johnny. And there was Johnny Kellog. Nineteen. He had married Johnny Gaston's pretty sister, Sidney. Taken her away from Thomas R. Miller. Miller was middle-aged. The wealthiest man in Gonzales. And now the three were gone, and Sidney had lost a brother, a husband, and . . . .

"The others from Gonzales—Albert Martin? Robert White? Isaac Baker?"

Susanna repeated the nod of her head. "All dead."

"Jacob Darst?"

The woman's shrug proved that it was needless to call off any more names. The Texians were dead.[56]

It was almost midnight when the small band arrived in Gonzales, finding the town in turmoil. Only ten days earlier, 32 of the Gonzales men had embraced their families, mounted their horses, and ridden off to aid the Alamo defenders; now 20 widows and their orphaned children would remember the fall of the Alamo as a turning date in their lives. R. E. Handy, described the scene:

> For four and twenty hours after the news reached us not a sound was heard save the wild shrieks of women and heart rending screams of their fatherless children.

Creed Taylor, Josiah Taylor, and several other men left Houston's camp to reconnoiter. As Creed described the occasion:

> That night was very dark, and as we groped our way toward camp our attention was suddenly attracted by a flare of lights in the direction of Gonzales, tall spires of flame shooting up now and then far above the horizon and illuminating the landscape in every direction. Hastening forward we soon arrived upon the scene and learned the cause of the phenomenon.

> Imagine, if you can, our utter bewilderment at finding the town in flames and our army camp deserted, with not a soldier in sight, save a few scouts who, like us, had not been called in from their posts of duty. The terrible story of the

Alamo fight told by Mrs. Dickerson had caused great excitement and the army and the citizens had literally stampeded.[57]

What had caused the citizens of Gonzales to "stampede" were not reports that the Alamo had fallen but the rumor that a force of 2000 Mexicans was marching toward the village.[58]

Little groups of men might be seen in various corners of the town, brooding over the past and speculating on the future, but they scarce spoke above a whisper, for here the public and private grief was alike heavy; it sunk deep into the heart of the rudest soldier.[59]

J. H. Kuykendall adds details in his account of Gonzales after the arrival of Mrs. Dickinson:

Superadded to this news, a rumor became rife that two thousand of the enemy—the advance division of the Mexican army—might be hourly expected at Gonzales. As may reasonably be supposed this news produced excitement in our camp. In the little village of Gonzales the distress of the families was extreme.[60]

Houston had been in the Gonzales camp but 52 hours. He was walking alone several hundred yards from camp when Karnes returned. At eight that night, the Dickinson party arrived, and Susanna sobbed out her story "of the butchering and burning, with some of the most stirring details."[61]

Soldiers in camp heard of the story. "The wildest consternation spread through the camp. Their alarm soon reached a pitch of desperation. Some were stunned with silence—other were wild with lamentations . . . ."[62]

Houston read the letter from Santa Anna and minutes later ordered Col. Burleson to break camp. At 8:30 he decided his troops should be prepared to break camp within three hours and to march to a camp near Burnham's Ferry on the Colorado.[63]

While camped at Navidad, March 15, 1836, Gen. Sam Houston prepared a report to James Collinsworth, chairman of the military committee:

Sir: Since I had the honor to address you from Gonzales, the lady of Lieutenant Dickinson, who fell at the Alamo, has arrived, and confirms the fall of that place, and the circumstances, pretty much as my express detailed them. She returned in company with two negroes—one the servant of Colonel Travis, the other a servant of Colonel Almonte.[64]

At least one other person left record of having talked with Susanna Dickinson soon after the fall of the Alamo—William Parker, who had set out from Nacogdoches to learn of the fate of his son.[65] On April 29, Parker, in Natchez, addressed a letter to the editor of *Free Trader*:

My informant states, that on his way in, he saw and conversed with Mrs. Dickinson, the widow of one of the guners at the fall of the Alamo, and the only white person in the fortress at the time of the final catastrophe of this post, who was spared by the enemy, and permitted to return into the American settlements. He says that Mrs. D informed him, that of the five who, for a moment survived their companions, and threw themselves on the victor's clemency, two were pursued into her room, and subjected in her presence to the most torturing death. They were even raised on the points of the enemy's lances, let down and raised again and again, whilst invoking as a favor, instantaneous death to terminate their anguish, till they were at least too weak to speak, and then expired in convulsion.[66]

INSCRIPTION
ON THE
SOUTH FRONT.
———
BE THEY
ENROLLED
WITH
LEONIDAS
IN THE
HOST
OF THE
MIGHTY
DEAD.

MARCH
6TH
1836
A. D.

Travis.

INSCRIPTION
ON THE
EAST FRONT.
———
Thermopylæ
HAD HER
MESSENGER
OF
DEFEAT,
BUT THE
ALAMO
HAD NONE.

MARCH
6TH
1836
A. D.

Bowie.

INSCRIPTION
ON THE SHAFT.
NORTH FRONT.
———
TO THE
GOD
OF THE
FEARLESS
AND FREE
IS
DEDICATED
THIS
ALTAR
MADE FROM
THE RUINS
OF THE
ALAMO

MARCH
6TH
1836
A. D.

Crockett

INSCRIPTION
ON THE
WEST FRONT.
———
BLOOD OF
HEROES
HATH
STAINED ME
LET THE
STONES
OF THE
ALAMO
SPEAK
THAT THEIR
IMMOLATION
BE NOT
FORGOTTEN.

MARCH
6TH
1836
A. D.

Bonham.

THE FOUR SIDES OF THE FIRST ALAMO MONUMENT THAT STOOD IN THE CAPITOL AT AUSTIN, AND WHICH WAS DESTROYED IN THE FIRE WHEN THE CAPITOL BURNED IN 1881.

52

CHAPTER FOUR

HOUSTON

MAGNOLIA, oak, pine, ash, sweetgum and cedar forests pushed against the steep banks of Buffalo Bayou. Limbs cernuous with gray Spanish moss sometimes dipped into the murky dark green waters or brushed palmettos and hyacinths at the water's edge.

A trail which touched Buffalo Bayou was destined to become Main Street, for a promotion campaign was underway to make this site the capital of the Republic of Texas. The Allen brothers—Augustus Chapman and John Kirby—purchased the league and a half of land. Five days later their advertisement appeared in the *Telegraph and Texas Register*, published at Columbia. The Allens boasted of the pine, ash, cedar and oak "in inexhaustible quantities," of the "tall and beautiful magnolia . . . in abundance," of "the rich lands" and of the "location at a point on the river which must ever command the trade of the largest and richest portion of Texas." And the Allens predicted that their proposed town just might become "the greatest interior commercial emporium" of the new nation.

Mrs. Dilue Harris recalled that three young men and her brother went in search of the advertised town. Of the incident, she wrote:

After being absent some time they said it was hard work to find the city in the pine woods, and that, when they did it consisted of one dugout canoe, a bottle gourd of whiskey and a surveyor's chain and compass, and was inhabited by four men with ordinary camping equipment.[1]

The town of Houston existed only in the dreams of the Allen men, for sweetgum woods remained to be cleared, swamps drained, and mosquitoes and snakes eradicated. There was work to do, and John Allen, "a very bright, quick man, with much magic about him,"[2] set about it. A member of the Republic's Congress, assembled in Columbia, Allen was determined to convince legislators that Houston should be the new center of the Republic. He invited solons to crowd around a sketch showing plans for the proposed city on exhibit in the Senate Chamber. Houston was, Allen insisted, "the most eligible place for the seat of government."

Naturally, other legislators had other proposals—Brazoria, Washington-on-the-Brazos, and even Nacogdoches, the congressman's home district. "Some sixteen locations[3] were proposed and there was acute rivalry among the proponents of the different sites." Yet, on the fourth roll call ballot, "a bare majority of twenty-one votes" favored Houston, a vote ratified Dec. 15. "The president," therefore, was authorized "to cause to be erected a building, suitable for the accommodation of the congress of the republic and such other buildings as may be necessary." The sum appropriated, Congressmen specified, should not exceed fifteen thousand dollars.[4]

Soon, plans owned by the Allen Brothers had land designated "Congressional Square," "Courthouse and a School House Square," and lots set aside as "Church Reserve." The map began to take on the appearance of a community; actual conversion on the ground was slower. Francis Richard Lubbock, who arrived on the scene in December, 1836, found a cluster of several small tents and a larger one serving as a saloon. "Several houses were in the course of erection," he recalled. "Logs were being hauled in from the forest for a hotel to be erected . . . . A small number of workmen were preparing to build cabins, business houses, and this hotel."[5]

The advertisement and the selection of the site as political center of the Republic pulled a number of persons to Houston, and they began arriving in covered wagons, steamboats, and on horseback. One visitor reported:

> Houses could not be built near as fast as required, so that quite a large number of linen tents were pitched in every direction over the prairie, which gave the city the appearance of a Methodist campground. Some of the tents, such as were used for groceries, were calculated to surprise one from their great size. A number of them measured more than a hundred feet in circumference, with conical tops, thirty or forty feet in height, supported by means of poles in the center.[6]

Among the 400 to 500 persons settling in the town were Susanna Wilkerson Dickinson, widow, and her young daughter, Angelina. Just when she arrived in Houston has not been recorded,[7] but she found the town filled with veterans of the Revolution waiting for their pay in military scrip or land.[8]

Although the town was filled with veterans of the Texas Revolution, Susanna Dickinson may have felt that she had few friends. At 3 p.m. Tuesday, Oct. 18, 1836, members of the House of Representatives meeting in the first session of the first Congress,[9] listened attentively as George W. Wright, presented a petition.[10] The petition concerning Susanna was referred to the committee on claims and accounts.

On Monday, Nov. 7, the House was in session. Thomas Jefferson Green, the representative from Bexar County,[11] presented the petition on claims and accounts against the Government of Texas and he moved that they be referred to the standing committee on claims and accounts. Representatives approved.

John Wheeler Bunton,[12] a member of the select committee, asked for the floor. He delivered the report from his group:

Mr. Speaker:
> I am authorized to make the following report after having had the claims & c of Mrs. Dickinson, with the report of the committee on claims and accounts, and also the joint resolution, under due consideration, your select committee, to whom was referred, by leave to report, that

said account cannot be allowed to Mrs. Dickinson as reported by said committee, but that said account ought to be allowed to the successors of the late lieutenant Dickinson, according to the laws now in force. This opinion is predicted upon the broad and plain principle that, it might be a perversion of the effects belonging to the succession of said lieutenant Dickinson, and that it would be an unconstitutional interference of Congress, to settle successions in the manner proposed.

On motion the joint resolution allowing Mrs. Dickinson, widow of the late lieutenant Dickinson, who fell gallantly defending the *Alamo*, a donation of five hundred dollars for his and her child's use and support, your committee would state, that, if said donation be given, Congress will be under like obligation to provide for the support of the widows of all who have fallen or who may fall in the war; many of whom no doubt are in a more helpless condition than the applicant in question; but in our present embarrassed situation we should first pay our just debts, before we make liberal donations, we should be just before liberal, your committee would therefore say unhesitatingly, that it would be highly impolitic to make the said appropriation.

Bunton took his seat, and John G. Robison, representative from Colorado County, moved that the report be adopted. Before the matter could go to a vote, Robison withdrew his motion.[13]

Branch Archer[14] jumped to his feet to move to recommit the report to the same committee with instructions to divide the question and report separately. Sensing that his motion was not popular, Archer withdrew it.

The congressman from Austin County, Mosely Baker, moved the measure be tabled. The motion carried.[15]

Where Susanna lived as well as when she arrived remain a mystery, but ''on or about the twenty-seventh day of November, 1837'' she was ''lawfully married to one John Williams.''[16]

Who was John Williams? *The Handbook of Texas* identifies one John R. Williams as a member of the Old Three Hundred, those settlers who made their homes in Stephen F. Austin's first colony. Williams received title to a league and a labor of land on July 24, 1824. In December, 1830, the *ayuntamiento* assembled at San Felipe to investigate titles and learned that Williams had located his land on Clark Creek but had not cultivated his league. He had, however, tilled his labor for a time but had deposed of it and had left the area in 1825.[17] The Republic of Texas Census for 1840 shows a John Williams living in Brazoria. He owned a town lot in Columbia, three slaves, and a gold watch.[18] Another John Williams who owned a saddle horse, resided in Fort Bend at the time.[19]

The marriage between Susanna and Williams may have been a contracted one, yet Susanna Williams inked her mark to a document certifying that from the time of the marriage ''until on or about the first of May or June eighteen hundred and thirty seven, she lived and cohabited with the said Williams as his wife, and was owned and acknowledged by him as such, and so deemed and respected by her neighbors and acquaintances, and although by the laws of God as well as by their mutual vows they were inseparable from the marriage state.'' Susanna, however, complained that ''John Williams has offered such indignities to the person of your petitioner as to render her condition intolerable and her life burthensome, and thereby forced her for her safety to leave his company.''

That the marriage was tempestuous, Susanna offered more proof through the words of her legal adviser:

> Our petitioner further sheweth unto your Honor that at the time she married the said John Williams she was the widow of Almeron Dickinson who was murdered by the Mexicans in the Alamo and had one child, who was dependent of the cruelty and barbarity which said Williams inflicted on your petitioner to such a degree as to produce or cause an abortion.[20] He also abused and beat the child of your petitioner beyond endurance.

> And your petitioner further sheweth under your Honor, that the said John Williams not only entirely refused to provide the necessary food to secure life but was careless

and inconsiderate about the welfare and comfort of his family.

And in due consideration of the premises, she prays that your Honor may grant her your process to cause the said Williams to be and appear at the next Term of your Honor's Court and to answer this petition and such other and further relief as shall to your Honor seem just, and as is duty bound will ever pray.

E. H. Winfield, clerk,[21] signed a statement that Susanna Williams appeared before him and took an oath that the facts were ''just and true, and that this affidavit is not made out of levity, but in sincerity and truth.'' The divorce, one of the first in the country, was granted March 24, 1838.[22]

Two months before the divorce was granted, Susanna—then a bride of only five months—may have attended the celebration marking the first anniversary of the Battle of San Jacinto. In mid-afternoon residents assembled around the ''Freedom Pole,'' raised on Main Street. Susanna may have felt uneasy moments when officials nervously attempted to get the silk flag up the staff. The rope slipped from the pulley. A bare chested man volunteered to climb the staff. When he failed, he turned over the duty to a sailor. President Sam Houston rewarded the sailor with title to a town lot. And the flag fluttered as the parade passed in review.[23]

Certainly, Susanna—young with shining black hair and sparkling blue eyes the shade of water hyacinths that choked the Bayou—received one of the invitations printed on white satin and requesting her presence at the San Jacinto Ball. Young ladies from as far away as Caney Creek and Onion Creek accepted invitations delivered by men on horseback, invitations designed to swell the female population of Houston for the occasion. President Sam Houston, his six foot two inch frame in ''black silk velvet, gold lace, crimson vest, cravat and silver spurs,'' appeared with a military plume stuck jauntily in his hat. Still nursing his San Jacinto wound, Houston wore red-topped boots. When the band—a violin, bass viol, and fife—struck up ''Hail to the Chief,'' Houston bowed before Mrs. Mosely Baker and invited her to be his dancing partner.[24] Houston, wearing black and crimson, and Mrs. Baker, in a white satin gown with black lace overdress, whirled about the floor, soon joined by other couples.

When the ball concluded, the men, many of them wearing white dancing slippers with their black frock-tail suits or blue broadcloth uniforms, escourted their ladies, some wearing decollete white dresses and shoes with French heels, to the hotel owned by Captain Ben Smith for a supper of "turkey, venison, coffee cakes, and sparkling wine."[25]

Guests were especially interested in "a number of wooden chandeliers suspended from the floor beams overhead" and holding hundreds of lighted sperm candles.[26]

By late April, 1837, the city contained more than 100 finished houses and more than 1,500 residents.[27] A large round tent served as a saloon, and Houstonians had plenty of "John Barley Corn and cigars." John Allen's "commodious building" to be used by the government was "raised, covered, and partly weather-boarded."[28]

Late autumn found the "peach blossom" capitol still unfinished; torrential rains damaged part of the building and disrupted Congress. One visitor wrote his wife, "I am badly situated here, the room that I occupy has no fire and I all most frose last night."[29]

How Susanna fared, readers can only guess.

Legends persist that for a time, Susanna lived in the Mansion House, managed by Pamelia Mann. Situated on two lots on the northeast corner of Congress and Milam streets, across from Congress Square, the Mansion Houe opened sometime in May, 1837, "A commodious, two-storied, plastered building with porches," Mansion House was the center of much activity in Houston. Its parlour was furnished with a sofa, a cherry center table, an eight-day clock, and half a dozen chairs. A pair of spittoons kept one of the seven slaves occupied when tobacco chewers fell short of their mark.

The dining room contained two long tables with benches. Above each table were flybrushes and at meal times Phill and

Maria kept them swinging with motions that were lulling to dining guests but disruptive to flies. An assortment of china and German silver cutlery remained on the tables, as did casters. Diners could order coffee, served from urns, or tea, served from britannia pots that many guests took to be pewter, or hard liquor and wine from crystal decanters. Black serving girls shuttled at least half a dozen 20-gallon coffee pots between the dining tables and the stoves, for coffee kept many Texians operating.

The kitchen, in a separate building, was furnished with a stove, corn and coffee mills, grinding stones, pots, pans, venison covers, bowls and other serving dishes.

On the second floor of Mansion House were the sleeping accommodations, three rooms with washstands, mirrors, and beds. Some rooms were arranged like dormitories containing double and single beds, ''with good mattresses, feather pillows, mosquito bars, and marseilles spreads.'' Calico rugs were spread throughout the hostelry, and in cold weather visitors huddled against the three cast and sheet iron stoves. Each room was furnished with curtains and mosquito bars.[30]

Pamelia Mann, owner of the hostel, was well-known throughout the Republic, and whether Susanna Dickinson lived in Mansion House or not, she doubtless knew Mrs. Mann as a woman who ''could drive oxen, fork a broncho and wield a bowie knife or a derringer,'' and she no doubt heard Houstonians boast that Pamelia had ''fought everyone except the Indians.''[31]

Mrs. Mann died Nov. 4, 1840, and if Susanna Dickinson lived in Pamelia's Mansion House, it was between May, 1837, and November, 1840.

By September, 1839, the capitol building was ''desolated and empty'' like a ''banquet hall deserted.'' Thirty teams and wagons were contracted to haul the papers, records and furniture to Austin, the permanent capital, and old timers could not refrain from mentioning that only three years earlier, the Texas archives had been hauled in a saddlebag. It had cost Texians $1,100 to have the government red tape carted off to the new community on the Colorado River.[32]

Although the Allen brothers had declared "there is no place in Texas more healthy, having an abundance of excellent spring water, and enjoying the sea breeze in all its freshness," Houston developed yellow fever, "the formerly so animated streets were deserted by people; all the shops are closed."[33]

It may have been that during this time, as Ed Kilman, columnist for the Houston *Post* once explained it, that Susanna was running her own boarding house at Franklin and Crawford,[34] only a few blocks from the boisterous, rowdy Mansion House.[35] Whether Susanna prepared meals for boarders or limited her culinary arts to satisfying appetites of members of her family, she probably talked about prices: a sack of corn for $3, flour at $17 a barrel, sugar at $45 a barrel, bacon at 38 cents a pound—and Susanna was especially fond of bacon—a bushel of potatoes, $3, and if she bought a spelling book for young Angelina, 50 cents. A pair of shoes for herself, Susanna found, cost $1.50.[36]

Bakers in the fall of 1839 quit making bread, and the *Morning Star* editorialized, "They can't do as well at Austin as we can here, if flour is seventy dollars a barrel."[37] Susanna, like other residents of Houston, no doubt, was concerned about the moving of the capital.

The editor of the *Telegraph and Texas Register* insisted that the "impression which prevails throughout the country that this city is exceedingly unhealthy" was "wholly false."[38] Not all residents, obviously, agreed, for there were pleas to improve sanitation. Francis R. Lubbock speculated that much of the sickness among members of Congress was caused "from the use of the bayou water," and he proposed:

. . . if they would furnish me with $500 I could procure for them in a very few days from New Orleans, cypress cisterns with the capacity of 10,000 gallons, and that would afford them with an abundance of good drinking water, healthy and palatable. My offer was accepted, and the cisterns were received and put up promptly. In a few days they were filled with excellent water, which had a fine effect upon the health of the members and proved a great benefit.[39]

The project was not carried out as hastily as Lubbock would imply. President Houston on Dec. 18, 1838, approved the act authorizing Lubbock to buy the cisterns,[40] but several months probably passed before they were installed. W. Y. Allen, who reached Houston March 31, 1838, said:

> Then the Houston waterworks was a cart with a large vessel which brought water from the Bayou and sold it by the bucket full. Occasionally there was a large vessel under the eaves of the house; there was a large one at the Capitol, where we were glad to get a drink of rainwater until the wiggletails would get too thick; we liked rainwater better than that from the Bayou.[41]

It was in the summer of 1838 that Beauchamps Spring on a tributary of White Oak Bayou[42] was discovered, a mile and a half north of Buffalo Bayou.[43] A Kentuckian, ''an old fox,'' Beauchamp purchased the area surrounding the Springs when he convinced the owner that he wanted a spot for his grave and some land around it. After he had the 50 acres, the new owner laid out Beauchampville, and before long lots were selling. ''Canvas tents, bush tents, board houses, waggons, and horses, negroes, white men, women and children, were promiscuously scattered from Houston to the spring, and two straight rows of houses were built in the pine forest, before yet the timber had been cut from the main street—Beauchamp Street.''[44] With the completion of a bridge over Buffalo Bayou, the spring offered Houstonians an ''inexhaustible supply of pure cola and wholesome water.''[45]

One of the men who may have found employment following this discovery was Francis P. Herring, water carrier, engaged in hauling water from Beauchamps Spring to Houston and selling it for seventy-five cents per thirty-gallon barrel.[46] Sometime late in 1838, the Houston Water-Works Company was organized. In December, the company passed a resolution that a competent person be named to determine the quality of water available at Beauchamp's, the size of engine that would be needed to bring the water to the city, the size of pipes, and the type of tanks needed for storage.[47]

Plans for the project did not materialize, and Houston continued to rely on cisterns and wells.

The meeting of Susanna and Herring is unrecorded, but on Dec. 20, 1838, they exchanged marriage vows.

While the county was still named Harrisburg, Herring appeared before a clerk who wrote, "to any judge, justice of the peace or minister of the gospal." He later inserted "regularly ordained" before the word "minister" before continuing:

Greetings: Know ye, that whereas E. P. Herring having this day produced satisfactory proof at this office that there exists no legal objections to he entering into a marriage contract with Mrs. Susana Dickinson.

You are therefore hereby summoned to unite them in matrimony according to _____ and make due return hereof within 60 days.

The man underscored his title with a flourish.

That night Herring and Susanna exchanged marriage vows before John Shaw, justice of the peace.[48]

Little is known about the man Susanna took as her third husband. A terse obituary in the *Telegraph and Texas Register*, September 27, 1843, states simply:

Died in this city on the 15th inst. of digestive fever, Francis P. Herring, formerly of Georgia.

A relative, however, has been quoted as saying, "He died of drink, not water."[49] And on July 7, 1847, a Third Class Headright File, No. 49, Harris County, was issued for 640 acres to Francis P. Herring, deceased. The certificate was delivered to George P. Carodine, to whom Herring had assigned rights Sept. 7, 1839.

A new decade brought new hopes for Houston and Susanna. One visitor reported that near Natchitoches, La., were wagon loads of families waiting to cross the Sabine River. The ferry was working night and day. In Houston, optimistic merchants were building brick walks in front of their stores.[50] On Feb. 16, 1846, President Anson Jones lowered the flag of the Texas Republic; the United States stars and stripes climbed the mast. Texas was no longer a separate nation but a part of the union.

The German, Ferdinand Roemer, arriving in Houston that year, noticed ''a number of men, evidently farmers, clad mostly in coarse woolen blanket-coats of the rightest colors—red, white and green.'' They were discussing the annexation of Texas.[51] The visitor also noticed the number of saloons, writing:

Some of them (considering the size of the City) were really magnificent when compared to their surroundings. Upon passing through large folding doors, one stepped immediately from the streets into a spacious room in which stood long rows of crystal bottles on a beautifully decorated bar. These were filled with divers kinds of firewater—among which, however, cognac and brandy were chiefly in demand.[52]

Susanna, like Texas, found a new union. She and Peter Bellows[53] obtained a license for their marriage signed by W. R. Baker, clerk, and dated Dec. 1847. On Dec. 15, the two—Peter, a 37-year-old native of Pennsylvania, and Susanna a 40-year-old Tennessean[54]—appeared before the Rev. Charles Gillett, an Episcopal minister, to repeat their vows.[55]

On May 5, 1845, Bellows appeared before members of the Houston council, and they granted him a license to operate one dray for a year. He paid a $15 fee.[56] The census for 1850 suggests that he did well. His occupation was listed as drayman and his real estate was valued at $1,000. Living in the Bellows' home when the census taker called were Susanna, aged 43; Angelina E. Dickinson, 16, with real estate valued at $2,000, and R. E. Goodbaker, a 20-year-old female born in Germany.[57] It is possible that Bellows was the same person identified by newsmen as Peter Belles, a candidate to represent Harris County in the state legislature. Opposing him in the 1851 election were Benjamin F. Tankersley, Francis Moore, Jr.,[58] John Green, Jr., and James W. Scott.[59]

Dr. Rufus Burleson had been a pastor in Houston almost a year. Someone complained to him that while the Baptist church might be the largest in the city, it could be the most fashionable if the minister would change his approach. In response, Burleson advertised one day in 1849 that he would preach on the mission of the church, using as his text, ''I came not to call the righteous, but sinners to repentance. I came to save that which is lost.''

When Dr. Burleson, his gray beard and mustache neatly trimmed, his watch chain shining but his eyes appearing sad, walked to his pulpit, he was aware of the packed church. ''The whole house and aisles and gallery were all crowded with eager listeners,'' he wrote later.

Following his sermon, Dr. Burleson walked to the front of the pulpit to invite the church to join him in prayer that ''God would save the worst sinners in Houston to demonstrate the wisdom and power of Christ to save.'' As Dr. Burleson described the situation later:

The vast congregation silently retired, deeply impressed with the great theme and glorious mission of the church. The next Wednesday night at prayer meeting I saw five or six persons weeping under deep conviction, and then, according to my custon, I invited all who wanted to be saved to come forward for special prayer.

Among those who came forward with tears and penitential sobs, was Mrs. Dickenson, who had become Mrs. Bells. She was nominally a member of the Episcopal Church, but with many tears she said she never knew anything about her lost condition or the true mission of the church, till she heard that sermon on Sunday night. I visited her at her home, and wept and prayed with her. I found in her a great bundle of untamed passions, devoted in her love and bitter in her hate. After many tears and prayers and religious instruction, she was joyfully converted. In less than two months her change was so complete as to be observed by all her neighbors. At least 1,500 people crowded the Banks of Buffalo Bayou on Sabbath evening to see her baptized. During all my pastorate in Houston, and especially during the cholera epidemic, she was a zealous co-laborer of mine in every good work. Whenever she did wrong, especially in giving way to passion, she would confess and weep over it.[60]

Memories of her days in the Alamo kept coming back—recalled by odors—like tacos or tortillas prepared over open braziers filled with purple hot coals—by sounds—musket shots and groans of men in pain—and often revived by white sheets of paper covered with quilled strokes that were read to her. She and her daughter received Donation Certificate No. 931 for 640 acres of land, signed by the Secretary of War Aug. 1, 1839. And in June, 1855, she and Angelina received a bounty warrant for 1920 acres in Clay County.[61]

Although the Republic of Texas on Dec. 21, 1837, had provided for donation certificates of 640 acres to all persons who had participated in the Alamo defense, many descendants had delayed making application for the grants. Then they appealed to Susanna for proof of service, and each request sent probes into her mind.[62]

Susanna's memories of the Alamo were revived on Dec. 9, 1850, when she was asked to certify that David P. Cummings had been one of the Alamo heroes. Heirs had filed for a grant of land, and Susanna's testimony was required. The clerk jogged Susanna's recollections by sharing the information he had concerning Cummings.

A scarcity of paper and the problems of getting settled into a new area had prevented Cummings from writing his father,[63] in Lewistown, Pennsylvania, but on Jan. 30, 1836, while in Gonzales, he began a letter telling how a month earlier he had arrived at the mouth of the Brazos in a vessel from New Orleans. He had walked from San Felipe to Gonzales, leaving his trunk with books and two rifles with a Mr. White at Columbia, 10 miles above Brazoria. Earlier, he had sold his best rifle for $30 and he had seen Sam Houston. Houston had advised the young man to get a horse and go to Goliad, saying he would see him there in a short time. And Cummings planned to connect himself with a company of Rangers or to go to San Antonio until he could connect himself with the army, "or regain my senses."

"Every man in this country at this time has to go upon his own foot as the government at present is unable to make any provisions for the Army," he wrote his parent, but he predicted a change for the better soon.

"Provisions are very scarce here and travelling or living is attended with considerable expense—all owing to the great number of volunteers from the United States besides the Emigration of Families into the Upper Colonies is unprecidented for the last five months," he continued in his letter. "Tho under rather indifferent circumstances myself at this time, I have no reason to complain of my coming to this country as I find nothing but what might have been expected; on the contrary I have the satisfaction of beholding one of the finest countries in the world . . . ."

On Feb. 14, 1835, Cummings again wrote his father, this time from San Antonio. He explained that as soon as he had posted his letter in Gonzales, he had left for San Antonio, where a sudden attack was expected, "ye and assistance was called for." He assured his father that nothing had happened. The enemy had not yet crossed the Rio Grande 180 miles away. Cummings urged his father to come look over the Texas territory.

After Susanna heard the brief summary of the letters Cummings had penned his father, her memory pricked, she could tell the clerk, "David P. Cummings and others with him came to and joined the garrison about three or four weeks before the taking of the same by the Mexicans."

Susanna had a distinct recollection of Cummings—"from his having been a surveyor and from his having company with others on permission went to Cibola to survey the head-rights and from his returning in a few days in compliance with an order (sent by express) from Col. Travis, and also from his having boarded with me and having me take care of his clothes."

When the clerk had prepared the deposition, he handed the paper to Susanna, who added her X to the line indicated for the mark of Susanna Bellows. The paper was dated Dec. 9, 1850.[64]

How unfortunate that no guest register exists of those boarders who ate at Susanna's table, that there is no roll of those who sat at her table when as a bride she began serving meals in the woods near Bolivar, Tennessee, of those who broke bread with her and her family in Gonzales, of those who put their feet under the oak *mesa* in the rock *casa* she and Almeron rented in San Antonio, and of those who ate heartily from her spread in Houston.

Sometime in 1851, a man of average height—probably 5 foot 11 inches, took his seat at Susanna's table in Houston. His blue eyes inventoried the food before him—black-eyed peas floating chunks of pork, cucumber pickles, hot cornbread, ears of corn the color of sunshine, squash, wheels of tomatoes, and peach cobbler. He liked what he saw—the type of food his mother had spread before the family on the Montgomery County farm where he lived. Susanna sized up the boarder as a country man, a no-nonsense man.

Conversation brought out that John Maynard Griffith was a farmer who sometimes captained steamboats bringing bales of cotton to Houston. Family legend says that Susanna decided Griffith *was* the man for her daughter, and on July 8, 1851, Judge W. R. Baker, clerk, wrote the authorization for any "judge, justice of the peace or minister of the gospel" to "unite in the Holy Bonds of Matrimony Mr. John Maynard Griffith and Miss Angelina Elizabeth Dickinson." The endorsement, signed by Rufus C. Burleson, who underlined his name with a flourish, was returned to the clerk's office July 12, indicating that he had performed the ceremony in the Baptist church July 8.[65]

The Griffiths set up housekeeping on John Maynard's farm. While the bridegroom felt a pride in his holdings, the bride felt alien—a city girl in the country. As her husband had told her, Montgomery County had sandy land capable of producing a bale of cotton to the acre or 35 bushels of corn. Post oak, white ash, black walnut, hickory, magnolia, and some wild peach flourished. The lumber business was brisk, many of the logs finding their way to Houston. Fishing was for idling away hours. But Angelina wanted the excitement that she had left in bristling Houston.

On May 13, 1853, Angelina and John Maynard Griffith looked upon their first child, a son Angelina named for her father—Almeron Dickinson Griffith. Two years later, a daughter, Susanna Griffith, joined the family. In 1857, another son, Joseph Griffith, was born.

But the marriage was doomed. When Angelina and John Griffith had agreed to exchange wedding vows, they had invited the Rev. Rufus C. Burleson to officiate. About the event, he later wrote:

Under the well-meant, pious persuasions of her mother, she married a good, honest, hard-working Baptist man from the country, I shuddered to see two such uncongenial spirits united in marriage. Marriage for money, for position, for convenience, or from parental persuasion, are often fearful mistakes. Marriage should never be from anything but real love, springing from the heart, guided by the head and limited by conscience. When people marry where they do not love, they are apt to love where they have not married. Soon the vivacious city girl got tired of her country home and her amiable, plodding husband. Alienations, repinings and divorce followed. The mother's heart bled over the ruin of her child's happiness.[66]

Perhaps, the break-up came following a party at Cypress. As Willard Griffith Nitschke, a granddaughter, wrote in *Women in Early Texas*:

At the Cypress "blow out," John Maynard Griffith lost his patience with Angelina and the homeward trip was a nightmare for Angelina. With aching head and sore feet, she listened to her husband pound at the evils of drinking and dancing. They were divorced soon afterwards.

Almeron Dickinson Griffith went to live with his uncle, Joshua Griffith, and the two youngest children went to live with their grandmother Susanna.

About the Cypress affair, another source wrote:

Some two or three years later I again met the "Babe of the Alamo." She did not look so fresh and attractive as when I first met her at the great fete. Her greeting was less cordial, and shadows were lurking on the surface of the broad, smooth, open forehead. An anxious, and at times a pained, expression would creep over her face, and there was a listlessness and signs of languor perceptible in the dark eyes—the rosy cheeks and lips were faded.[67]

On Nov. 21, 1853, a notary public of Harris County certified that Susanna Bellows had signed statements acknowledging that a man named Rose was in the Alamo during the battle. To the notary, J. Castanie, Susanna said, "Sometime during the years 1835 or 6 I lived with my former husband, Almeron Dickerson, in the town of San Antonio in the said state of Texas and that I was acquainted with a man by the name of Rose who with David Crockett was frequently an inmate of my home, and that when the army of Mexico advanced upon the town, said Rose and Crockett and all the Americans took refuge in the Alamo."

The words were Susanna's; the spellings Castanie's.

Susanna admitted that she did not remember the given name, but Rose must have been a man of some 30 years of age. He was of medium height and had a fair skin that was disposed to freckle. Sandy or light hair. Blue or gray eyes. His broad shoulders tended to round, to stoop. Rose, she believed, would have weighed between 150 and 160 pounds, and as nearly as she remembered, he came to Texas with his friend and companion, Davy Crockett.

After Castanie prepared the statement—using his own spelling for names—Susanna signed it with her mark.

"Mrs. Dickinson was a Mrs. Bellows, who for many years was a good and reputable citizen of Houston." So said a letterwriter in a piece of correspondence submitted for publication in the *Telegraph*.[68] Her husband, obviously, was not of the same mind, for through his lawyers, Henderson[69] and Johnstone, Peter Bellows petitioned T. W. Gray, judge of the Seventh Judicial District. Received for the spring term, 1857, the petition was against "Susannah Bellows, a citizen of Harris County temporarily residing in Caldwell County." Bellows alleged that:

. . . on or about the first day of December A. D. 1847 petitioner was married to the defendant, according to the laws of Texas, and that they lived together as man and wife, from said marriage, until sometime in the spring of A. D. 1854, when she left voluntarily, his bed and board, and remained in the West some four or five months, when she returned to the City of Houston, and again left and has remained separated from him ever since that time to the present, and he charges and alleges that the said defendant has voluntarily left his bed and board for the space of three years, with the intention of abandonment. He further charges and alleges, that on or about the time she left his bed and board in the County of Harris, in the City of Houston, she was guilty of adulting with several persons, whose names to your petitioner is unknown, he further charges and alleges that on or about the 1st day of October A. D. 1854, she took up her residence in a house of ill fame, in the City of Houston, and remained therein, as one of its inmates for the accomodation [sic] of the public, and whilst in said house, great numbers of men were in the habit of visiting said house, and he charges and alleges, for the space of three months, whilst in said house, she was in the constant habit of committing adultery with various persons, whose names to your petitioner was unknown. He further charges and alleges that the defendant taking up her residence in a house of ill fame as before alleged was such an outrage, upon his feelings as to render their living together as man and wife insupportable. Wherefore he sues and prays that she be abid to appear and answer this petition, and that upon a final hearing of this suit, your Honor will dicuo the bonds of matrimony heretofore existing between the petitioner and defendant, and be declared null and void, and dissolved, and for costs of this suit and as in duty bound he will ever pray.[70]

Minutes of the court show that on Monday, June 15, 1857, the plaintiff Peter Bellows was represented by his attorney, and the defendant, duly cited, ''came not but made defense.'' A jury of John Harmon, Robert Kelley, J. Morse, P. B. George,[71] Henry Trott, P. Milner, L. Milner, L. Pheland, G. Gerson,[72] John Revidam, E. Duly, and Jesse Thurman listened to the evidence. Their foreman then reported:

We the jury find the material allegations set forth in plaintiff's petition true and find for the plaintiff that the bonds of matrimony heretofore existing between the plaintiff Peter Bellows and the defendant Susannah Bellows be and the same are hereby forever dissolved and it is further ordered that the plaintiff have and recover of the defendant all costs in and about this suit expended.[72]

Lubbock (who later became governor) addressed the district court of Caldwell County, spring term, 1857:

You are hereby commanded to summon Susannah Bellows if to be found in your county, to be and appear at the District Court to be in and for the County of Harris, aforesaid, at the court house thereof, in the City of Houston, on the 7th Monday after the 1st Monday in April, A. D. 1857 . . . .[74]

The citation was delivered to S. H. Henderson, sheriff, on May 1, 1857, and he endorsed it:

Executed by Serving the within named Susannah Bellows in person with a certified Copy Petition accompanying the within with this 1st day of May, 1857.[75]

The divorce was granted, June 15, 1857, and sheriff Grymes was ordered to levy on Susanna's property the costs amounting to $14.90. He reported, however, "no property found in county belonging to defendant. Susan Bellows Removed to the City of Austin with all her effects and fixtures prior to reception of this (order)."[76]

CHAPTER FIVE

LOCKHART

Ox-drawn wagons loaded with crops bound for Lavaca and Alleyton clogged the dusty streets of the village of Lockhart. Already 18 business houses fringed the center of town, 15,505 slaves performed farm and domestic chores, and 15,244 cattle grazed on the prairie land around the cluster of buildings.[1] An immigrant, arriving in town in 1857, noted in his diary:

> Lockhart presents a very neat appearance situated in a live oak grove, an elevated prairie covered with short green grass, give it a much clearer appearance than most of the small towns we have passed through and being in hauling distance of the Bastrop Saw Mills, lumber costing delivered here but $40.00 PM which is considered cheap enough. The houses are generally of wood and are of a better style of building than most other places west.[2]

The same visitor expressed a belief that any immigrant interested in land should remain in the place twelve months, looking over the situation. He wrote:

> A family can be supported cheap here, the finest beef under the sun at 3 cents, meal 50 cents, groceries as low as we have them in Alabama.

One of the appeals of Lockhart was its water supply, about which the same visitor made this observation:

This is a finely watered place. We were taken around to the Springs in town, there cannot be less than 100 and very bold. At the branch of one there is now the timber laying for the purpose of laying an overshot mill, there being a fall of 20 feet or more, the owner designs bringing several of the spring branches together, which he can readily do and have as much power as he may want.

The springs which furnished Lockhart water were shaded by live oak, walnut, pecan and ''the tree that produces India rubber.''[3]

To this village Susanna Dickinson Bellows fled when she left Houston in a bouncing stage in 1857, and it was this place that marked the turning point in her life, when she left tragedy behind and became familiar with happiness and true love. Exactly when she arrived remains unknown, but Susanna relied on her knowledge of cooking to set up a boarding house.[4]

How and where Susanna and Joseph William Hannig became acquainted is disputed. Some sources say that the two met in Lockhart; some place the meeting in Houston, and still other sources suggest that the two were in New Orleans when their paths crossed. Born in Selesia, Germany, Hannig—a tall dignified man with a moustache—had arrived in this country only six years before he and Susanna exchanged wedding vows.[5] The Louis W. Kemp files suggest that Susanna was in New Orleans when she was introduced to Joseph William, ''a most worthy and industrious man who had been sent by Jefferson Davis to establish a workshop for the manufacturing of munitions of war.''[6] Yet, Hannig was a cabinetmaker; his brother Frank was a gunsmith. It was around Frank's shop—a shack in the yard of the Hannig home—that Susanna's grandchildren played when they came to visit their grandmother during her Lockhart residence. Similar statements were made by Elmer L. Callihan in a feature story for *The Dallas Morning News*.[7] Callihan wrote that Frank W. Hannig ''worked in the old gunshop,'' but he later confused Frank with Joseph William. Frank remained in Lockhart, and when he died in 1892, his tools were left in place as he last used them, ''open to inspection of the interested tourist.''

E. A. Masur, late Lockhart merchant gave the logical explanation. ''Hannig was a pioneer blacksmith, a man who really appreciated a good meal. When he sampled Susanna's cabbage, bacon, and cornbread, he just up and married her.[8]

The gun shop and the Hannig household were on Market Street, less than two blocks from the business district of Lockhart. Here in the residence, which later Lockhart residents called a "shanty" and "an eyesore," Susanna and Joseph were married by the Rev. J. H. Wells, Baptist minister.

Word soon reached Susanna that Angelina had delivered a son, this one named Joseph honoring Joseph Hannig. No doubt Susanna and the man rejoiced over the news. Susanna, no doubt, prayed that the new member of the family might tighten the bonds between the daughter and her "man from the country." Surely, Susanna felt joy that her daughter had seen fit to name the child in honor of the man Susanna had selected as her fifth husband.

Susanna Dickinson Hannig could not escape her past. Reluctant to talk about the Alamo because the topic seemed distasteful to her husband, Susanna could not ignore the queries that came to her, the pleas for help of descendants seeking proof that ancestors had fought in the old mission. The matter of Rose, about which Susanna had been questioned while she lived in Houston, was not settled, and on June 30, 1857, Sam J. R. McDowell, the clerk of the county court of Caldwell, where Susanna was living at the time, was commissioned to take depositions of the woman of the Alamo.

When McDowell called on her, he took his instructions from the envelope and glanced over them. In his own penmanship, the Commissioner of Claims at Austin had written, "The Commissioner will please certify to the identity and credibility of the witness if known to him. If the witness is unknown, he will require his identity and credibility to be established by the testimony of at least one credible witness, whom he does know and certify accordingly." Half aloud, more to himself than to Susanna, the clerk muttered, "No problem there since I've known you for some time." He then flipped the sheets of paper to one on which were numbered questions.

Directing his questions to Susanna, the Caldwell clerk, who because of his birth in Tennessee and his age, found he had much in common with the woman he interviewed, said, "You're accustomed to such questions, I guess, with a number of heirs now filing claims?"[9]

A warm nod and smile answered his question.

"Well, the heirs of James R. Rose, have called for a headright, bounty and donation claim of land. They say Rose was in the Alamo."

Susanna, folding her arms in her lap, nodded. She then said that she had once before completed a questionnaire about the man, but . . . .

"When did you migrate to Texas?"

Susanna, without hesitation, answered, "In the year 1833."

"Did you reside in the city of San Antonio de Bexar in the year 1835 and 1836? And were you residing there when the Mexican Army advanced upon the city in 1836?"

Obviously wearied by the same question that she had answered over and over, Susanna replied, "Yes" to both questions.

"During your residence in San Antonio de Bexar, did you know a person of the name of Rose, at that time with the Texas Army? If yes, did the said Rose join the late David Crockett to engage in the war between Mexico and Texas?"

"Yes, he did."

"Do you remember his Christian name?"

"James."

"At the time the Mexican Army advanced upon San Antonio de Bexar, did the said Rose with David Crockett and the other Americans take refuge in the Alamo and at that time was he the only person of the name of Rose in the Texas Army?"

"He did. Was the only man in the army by the name of Rose that I knew of."

"During your residence in San Antonio was the late David Crockett and the said Rose inmates of your house?"

Susanna shook her head to indicate that she remembered when Crockett and Rose visited her home.

"Were they on friendly terms?"

Again, with a shrug, Susanna answered, "Yes—so far as I knew, they were."

The clerk changed tone slightly as he switched from the question-answer approach, hoping to gain discussion from the woman. "State the age and personal appearance of the said Rose—the manner by which he came to his death and the facts you know in regard to him."

Susanna estimated Rose's age at between 35 and 40. "He was of medium height, heavy set, rather full square face, very quick spoken," she said.

Pausing, as if remembering what the other question was, Susanna then resumed speaking. "He fell with the rest of the defenders of the Alamo—during the siege. I saw Rose often, and upon one occasion he and my husband, Capt. Dickinson, spoke of a narrow escape Rose had made from a Mexican officer after that first attack."

Her eyes became misty—trying to remember details that she would like to forget.

After McDowell had completed the interview, he thanked Susanna and promised that he would recopy the answers and she could stop by the courthouse to add her signature.

It was July 16, 1857, before Susanna found it convenient to visit the "temporary frame" courthouse and enter the clerk's office. McDowell read the material to her and showed her where to sign. With the quill, she formed a small, neat X to the statement. McDowell changed the spelling of Susanna's name, inking over-*Bellows* to read *Bellis*. He then wrote that Susanna had appeared before him and answered questions, and in his presence had signed the document.

"I further certify that the said Susanna Bellis is the identical person referred to in this commission, that I am personally acquainted with her and believe the statements she has made are

entitled to full credence,'' he wrote. He spelled Susanna's name
Bellis in this statement.[10]

On March 28, 1854, in Houston, Peter Bellows, Angelina
Griffith and John M. Griffith, identified as heirs of Almeron
Dickinson, appointed Susanna their ''true and lawful agent and
attorney'' with power ''to settle, due for, demand and receive, be
sued, compromise, receipt for, bargain, sell, make titles to, and to
do any and all things in and about the Estate of the said Almeron
Dickinson.''[11] Using this power of attorney, Susanna on Sept.
20, 1856, sold to John S. McKean the land ''generally known as
the Dickerson league—being the location of a grant made by the
Mexican government to Amerion Dickerson in his lifetime (as a
Colonist in the Colony of Green DeWitt & one league in quantity).'' The property was described in this manner.

. . . (lying) on the North East margin of the San Marcos
river four leagues below the old Bexar road—beginning the
upper line on the bank where stands a stake for the lower
corner of survey No. two from which a Pecan 18 inches in
diameter bears South 53° West at 3½ varas distant and an
Elm 14 inches in diameter bears N25° West 6 varas.
Thence run North 50° East 5853 varas to land mark of the
North West corner a mesquit 10 inches in diameter bearing
from it North 62° East at 6 varas distant and another 8
inches in diameter bearing South 86° West at 6½ varas
distance. Thence South 40° East 5000 varas to where set a
land mark for the North East corner a mesquit 18 inches in
diameter bearing South 82° West at 6 varas distance Thence
toward the river South 50° West 5733 varas to the bank at a
place where stands a stake for the lower corner from which a
Spanish oak 18 inches in diameter bears South 86° West at
11½ varas distance and an Elm 12 inches in diameter bears
S85° West at 10 vrs distance which demarcations include
the meanders of the river, these amounting to 6680 varas
which complete the limits of the league aforesaid.[12]

With money that Susanna collected from the sale of land in
the original DeWitt grant, to Almeron Dickinson, she was able to
stake Joseph William Hannig in setting up a business in Austin.

78

The couple moved its meagre belongings to a house on Pine Street, between Neches and Red River. Hannig opened a cabinet shop in a frame building across the street from the Missouri Hotel, a two-story structure. Jotting from his building over the cobblestone walk, a sign proclaimed to Austinites that here were "England & Hannig, Cabinet Makers." The sign was anchored to the roof on one side and to a fancy dowel-like post at the edge of the street.

Mrs. Hannig tended her household chores, perhaps making a peach cobbler, her favorite dessert then strolled down the Avenue on a shopping expedition. Or, she walked to the cabinet shop to admire her husband's work. And they went across the street to the Missouri House to talk with visitors, Susanna hoping that no one would approach her for information about the Alamo.[13]

At least once again, Susanna was called upon to verify the presence of an individual in the Alamo, and Susanna again gave the clerk trouble with the spelling of her married name. He consistently went according to sound—Hunneck—yet on March 8, 1860, Susanna put her X to the document the clerk had prepared.

The statement followed the application of the heirs of Henry Warnell for bounty and donation lands, and Susanna vowed that she had known Henry and believed him to have been "among the unfortunate number who fell." She told the clerk, "I recollect having heard him remark that he had much rather be out in the open prairie than to be kept in that manner. Said Warnell was a man of rather small stature, light complexion, and I think red or sandy hair."[14]

The application for bounty lands was submitted by Henry's son, John, his sole heir. Henry's wife, Ludie Ragsdale Warnell, had died in giving birth to the son.[15]

Each request for statements must have galled Susanna, who heard pleas for aid from her own daughter draw dulcet, poetic entreaties but loud "nays" from members of the legislature. On Nov. 21, 1849, the House of Representatives in regular session heard a bill recommending aid for Angelina Elizabeth Dickinson, the "Babe of the Alamo." The measure recommended appropriating the "sum of one hundred and fifty dollars" annually for ten years "for the support and education" of Miss Dickinson. The bill was read a second time Nov. 22[16] and referred to the Judiciary Committee,[17] whose chairman was Georgia born, legally trained Benjamin Crowell Franklin.[18] Franklin's committee reported Dec. 13 with a substitution bill designed to relieve the woman's wants and to insure her education.[19] The following day the legislators adopted a substitute resolution and ordered it engrossed.[20]

On Dec. 18, a joint resolution, pointing out that " . . . whereas the information communicated to our Commander by said Widow (Susanna) was of uncalculable value, enabling him to prepare for defense . . . " recommended a sum of $300 a year be awarded the daughter of Capt. and Mrs. Almeron Dickinson. The sum would be paid for two years, would be drawn quarterly, and would be under the control of the chief justice of Harris County. After a third reading, the resolution received a "constitutional majority."

Sometime during the legislative process, Guy Morrison Bryan rose to his feet, looked directly toward Charles G. Keenan[21] and spoke:

I intended, Mr. Speaker, to be silent on this occasion, but silence would not be a reproach, when to speak is a duty. No one has raised a voice in behalf of this orphan child; several have spoken against her claim. I rise, sir, in behalf of no common cause. Liberty was its foundation, heroism and martyrdom consecrated it. I speak for the orphan child of the Alamo. No orphan children of fallen patriots can send a similar petition to this House—none save her can say, 'I am the Child of the Alamo.' Well do I remember the consternation which spread throughout the land, when the sad tidings reached our ears that the Alamo had fallen.[22] It was here that a gallant few, the bravest of the brave, threw themselves betwixt the enemy and the settlements, determined not to surrender nor retreat. They redeemed their pledge with the forfeit of their lives—they fell, the chosen sacrifice to Texas freedom! Texas, unapprised of the approach of the invader, was sleeping in fancied security, when the guns of the Alamo first announced that the Atilla of the South was near.[23]

Infuriated at the resistance of Travis and his noble band, he marshaled his whole army beneath the walls, and rolled wave after wave of his hosts against those battlements of freedom. In vain he strove—the flag of liberty—(Mexico's flag of 1824), still streamed out upon the breeze, and floated proudly from the outer wall. Maddened and persistent, he reared his batteries, and after days of furious bombardment, and repeated assaults, he took a blackened and ruined mass—the blood stained walls of the Alamo. The noble, the martyred spirits of all its gallant defenders, had taken their fight to another fortress not made with hands . . . but for this stand at the Alamo, Texas would have been desolated to the Sabine.

Sir, I ask this pittance, and for whom? For the only living witness, save the mother, of this awful tragedy—'this bloodiest picture in the book of time,' the bravest act that ever swelled the annals of any country, Grant the boon! She claims it as the Christian child of the Alamo—baptized in the blood of a Travis, a Bowie, a Crockett, and a Bonham. To turn her away would be a shame! Give her what she asks, that she might be educated, and become a worthy child of the State!—that she may take that position in society to which she is entitled by the illustrious name of her martyred father—illustrious because he fell in the Alamo.[24]

As Bryan took his seat, he probably puzzled how his speech had effected the Speaker of the House, who had once served as a U.S. Army surgeon among the Indians,[25] and he must have questioned whether his plea would nudge any of his fellow legislators.

English-born James Charles Wilson,[26] representing Brazoria in the legislature, also entreated the law makers to support the measure, saying:

. . . When the Alamo fell, a nobler than Leonidas,[27] a more devoted band than the Spartans, sank amid its ruins. They shed their blood for us—they poured out their lives as water for the liberties of Texas! and they have left us, of that bloody, yet glorious conflict, one sole memento—one frail, perishable keepsake—the child whose petition for assistance is before us. Shall we turn her away? Shall we say—"Though your father served the State in his life; though he fell in the ranks of those men whose names history shall chronicle and nations shall delight to honor; though you alone, of all the children of Texas witnessed that direful scene, whose bare contemplation makes the stout heart quail; though the credit and honor of Texas are alike concerned in taking care of your childhood and watching over your youth, in providing for your happiness and respectability; though you, the Babe of the Alamo, will be an object of interest to all who may visit our State in the after years, when the pen of the historian shall have recorded your connection with the early glories and sufferings of our now happy land—yet for all this, we will suffer you to grow up in uncultured wildness, in baneful ignorance, perchance in vice, rather than make this pitiful appropriation to enable you to render yourself capable of occupying that position in society to which you are in a peculiar degree entitled by the strange and thrilling circumstances surrounding your life. Sir, I trust such an act may not mar the history of Texas. Sure am I, by my vote it never shall. It is related of Napoleon, that when an officer whom he loved was wounded and, from the narrowness of the defile in which the conflict raged, was in imminent danger of being crushed to death by the feet of contending friends and foes, while the emperor looked on in deep anxiety for his fate, a female, an humble follower of the man, with a babe on one arm, pressed through the melee to the wounded man, and passing her other arm around him, conveyed him to a place of comparative safety near the emperor; but just as she turned away from the object of her daring and benevolent solicitude, a ball struck her dead at the feet of Napoleon. He, taking the motherless babe in his arms, called a grenadier, saying, "Bear this child to the rear, and see that it is well attended to, for henceforth it is the Child of the Empire." Mr. Speaker, the Child of the Alamo, is the Child of the State, and we cannot treat her with neglect without entailing lasting disgrace upon Texas.[28]

The joint resolution was received in the Senate on Dec. 19[29] and read for the first time. The second reading came on Dec. 20,[30] after which it was referred to the committee on finance. On Jan. 2, 1850, the chairman of that committee reported:

Many orphans were left in a more forlorn and dependent state that the one the bill is intended to relieve.

. . . If the finances of the state were in a condition to give a pension to all . . . the heirs of those who were killed, then would your committee treat the bill with more favor?

In a drawl of his native North Carolina, Uncle Jesse, as he was familiarly known, or "the ever faithful guardian of the Treasury"[31] as he was politically recognized, continued, "But as this is not the situation of our treasury, and as the subject of this relief does not appear to be in a distressed situation, but rather the reverse, being a young lady of some fifteen years of age, and entitled to the estate of her father, which consists of more than five thousand acres of land . . . ."[32]

The measure received an unfavorable vote.

If thoughts of the Alamo were revived with each application for a land grant, with each request for proof that an individual gave his life in the mission-fortress, Susanna's memories were jogged in other ways. One evening in 1862, Dr. Rufus Burleson and the Rev. W. W. Harris were conducting a revival service in the Baptist church. When Dr. Burleson invited to the altar all who had been converted and had once been members but had "grown cold and wandered away, and now wanted to return to the path of duty," he recognized an old friend as one of several who walked to the front of the church. As Burleson wrote:

. . . To my astonishment I saw the stalwart form moving up the aisle that I saw moving up the aisle in Houston in 1849.

Upon reaching the altar rail, Susanna Hannig extended her hand. "Erring and wayward, but still struggling to do right and serve my Redeemer," she told Dr. Burleson as the two shook hands. Susanna extracted a promise that he would call on her the next afternoon.[33]

This renewal of friendship with Dr. Burleson and Susanna's repledging of faith in religion may have prepared her for the word she received several years later. The death of her only daughter must have been a severe shock to Susanna.

Sources differ on details concerning Angelina Elizabeth Dickinson Griffith Holmes Britton's death. In a letter to L. W. Kemp, E. A. Masur of Lockhart says that "the Babe of the Alamo" died while visiting in New Orleans in 1870 and was buried there. The grave remains unmarked.[34] An entirely different account was published in *Flake's Daily Bulletin*, published in Galveston on Wednesday, July 14, 1869:

> What a pure fancy that saying is that 'Death loves a shining mask.' We fancy a most practical fancy, and this is that death is no respector of person, but high and low, virtuous and vile, feel his inevitable grasp and fall before his breath. But 'shining mask' may have a different signification from the ones we have attached to it. It may have reference to the spirit more than to the moral code as judged by the world, and while one's life may be like the corsair's name, 'linked with one virtue and a thousand crimes,' the one virtue may constitute the shining mask of the text and in the eyes of Heaven the soul thus styled may not be misnamed.

> But we intended to announce simply the death last evening of "*Em*. Britton," a name not unfamiliar to Texans, as being that of a woman connected forever with the struggle of the Republic at the Alamo, a Mrs. Robertson[35] and her only child, a daughter, were saved. This daughter was *Em*. Britton. "*Em* was made quite a heroine because of her romantic fate in early life, and we believe some grants of land were made to her. She grew up, was comely in face and person, and married a Mr. Britton.

We do not know how it happened that they parted, nor is it necessary to know, but she embraced the life of a courtezan and so died last night.

Her pilgrimage is done. Let us erect over her grave the words of a recently departed sister, Ada Menken: "Thou, God, Knowest."[36]

On Sunday, July 18, *Flake's Bulletin* mentioned in the mortuary report the name Emma Britton, aged 37, dead of uterus hemorrhage. Her place of birth was listed as Texas.

Susanna must have reflected on the life of her daughter—the babe who charmed Travis so that he put a string necklace around her neck while she played in the Alamo, the daughter who had won Santa Anna's heart so that he begged to adopt her, the child who found country life so alien that she left her first husband and children, who wooed Oscar Holmes in New Orleans and who became his wife in 1864, and the woman who later nursed victims of a Galveston plague. No doubt, Susanna tried to blot out some details—how Angelina could have left her children, whether she had legally become the wife of Jim Britton, and, no doubt, Susanna puzzled where she had gone wrong in rearing the vivacious beauty.

From the days she had opened her dining room to boarders, Susanna had managed business affairs, so it was not surprising to find her name on several documents in the deed records of Caldwell County. On Oct. 10, 1856, Susanna purchased from Marcus Trumble two town lots in Lockhart.[37] For the property she paid $160.

"Justly indebted to C. B. Maynard, John E. Clardy, and John G. Blanks in the sum of one hundred and forty six dollars and sixty cents by note," Susanna promised to pay "with ten per cent interest from maturity for value received this 26th Nov. 1857." She signed to Spencer Ford "for the purpose of securing the payment . . . and for further consideration of five dollars," she deeded lots 11 and 12.[38] Ford, on Feb. 1, 1858, signed a release reconveying title of the property to "Susannah Bellis now Susannah Hannig all of the property conveyed to me as trustee in said deed of trust."[39]

On Feb. 4, 1858, J. W. Hannig for consideration of $400 sold to Susannah A. Hannig "all of the following tracts or lots of land lying and being in the town of Lockhart, County and State aforesaid, viz: Lots No. three in block No. one, also Lot No. two in block No. one, both of which laid down in M. Trumbles plot of Lots." An old friend of Susannah's, Sam J. R. McDowell, county clerk, certified that the deed was filed in his office 2 p.m. Feb. 4.[40]

And on March 31, 1858, as "citizens of Travis County," Joseph Hannig and Susanna Hannig, his wife, accepted $250 from Frank Hannig for lots 2 and 3 in Block No. 1, Lockhart. These lots were situated "on the south side of San Antonio Street along with all the improvements and appurtenances." J. W. Hannig signed the deed, and Susanna placed her mark on the document.[41]

CHAPTER SIX

EARLY AUSTIN

AUSTIN, entering the 1870 decade, was growing—ready to leave the protective, motherly curve of the Colorado river, but prevented by that placid body of water stretching south and held from westward expansion by the steep, unapproachable limestone cliffs overhanging Shoal Creek. Augustus Koch prepared a map of the city in 1873, showing on the west the mansion of former Gov. and Mrs. E. M. Pease in a wooded area, and on the east the French Legation perched on a hill surrounded by only a sprinkling of houses. The artist sketched wagons and horses crossing the pontoon bridge at the foot of Brazos Street and a loaded flatboat sailing up the Colorado. At the mouth of Shoal Creek, he drew two covered wagons, each pulled by eight oxen and guarded by horsemen. As Koch saw the town, there were thick, high buildings on each side of Congress Avenue,[1] at the head of which was the limestone capitol, described by one critic as looking like a "large sized corn crib with a pumpkin for a dome."[2]

For Susanna and Joseph W. Hannig, the decade was one of business endeavor. Midsummer, the Hannigs paid $2000 to James Harrington for four lots in block 12. Notary Public James W. Smith, in preparing the deed transferring title to the property, stated that Mrs. Hannig signed her mark after he had talked privately with her.[3] She vowed that she had willingly signed the document. The following year Hannig purchased two blocks in the Connor's addition between Pine and Pecan, and he and five other businessmen invested $800 in lot 7, block 34.[4]

The Hannig holdings were growing, then something happened. On Oct. 25, 1872, for a dollar, Susanna signed to Eugene Bremond several parcels of property and "also all community interest in the stock of merchandise and furniture now owned and controlled by her husband and self with all merchandise and personal property which hereafter may be acquired during our matrimonial connection, to have and to hold the same real estate to Eugene Bremond, trustee, to the heirs of Joseph W. Hannig, forever."

Under terms of the agreement, Hannig would "exercise uninterrupted control of the community interest hereby conveyed in real and personal estates. Said J. W. Hannig shall sell, barter, and exchange said personal property without any permission by said trustee . . . Hannig is to convey property to whoever J. W. Hannig may designate." A provision was made that should Hannig "outlive his wife, the said Susanna A. Hannig," the property would be handled by the trustee. Should Mrs. Hannig survive her husband, "the trustee shall convey the said interest held in trust by him to her . . . during her life and to such persons as Joseph Hannig may designate by will after her death."

Notary James W. Smith conferred with Susanna, and in private she acknowledged that she "willingly signed and did not wish to retract" the sentiments of the document. She agreed that she had received $1 for herself and her grandchildren, Susan, Joseph, and Sallie Griffith; for some reason she made no mention of A. D. Then at 3 p.m. Oct. 26, 1872, she penned an X to the paper.[5]

Hannig, however, continued active in assuming mortgages on property. Before Swante Palm on Feb. 18, 1873, for instance, he assumed the mortgage on property held by W. F. Ford and wife.[6]

Land, Hannig must have reasoned, could only increase in value as the state's capital bristled with activity. He echoed the sentiments of a visitor from Houston, who, in 1874, said:

. . . The streets are literally thronged with vehicles of every description while a steady stream of wagons . . . is continually passing to and fro, lending vivacity and life to the scene.[7]

By 1874, the Austin City Railroad Company had been organized to bring horse-car transportation to the growing community. "The day for dragging and poking along," wrote a correspondent for the newspaper, "we hope is played out in Austin. We should not be surprised to see a mile of street railway in operation, by the first of November." Hannig, however, may have been among those property owners of Pecan Street who were not so enthusiastic about the laying of the iron rails. They wrote:

. . . As owners of real estate on Pecan Street, we hereby notify you that we consider your action . . . as an encroachment upon our private rights and as tending to depreciate the value of our property, and, by obstructing the street, to drive trade and travel away . . . .[8]

Austinites of the time expressed more than a stir of interest in horse racing. A track, judges stand, and grandstand advertised as "the finest in the South," decorated the growing Austin. Horsemen used the street, which became known as Speedway, as a warm-up track. The *Statesman* urged the Jockey Club to use more decorum in order to encourage the ladies to attend the races. Some women had left the grounds on one occasion because of some of the remarks made.[9] Interest in racing focused on some of the stables that were being built in Austin. Dr. William Copeland Philips raced Austin bred horses—at New Orleans and Charleston—and he had entered "Little Reb" and "Judge Hancock" at Savannah.[10]

While some Texans were building their stables, Hannig was adding to his collection of mortgages. A piece of property with 69 feet fronting Pine and running back 128 feet to the alley, was sold to John B. Costa, who, to secure payment, executed a note for $452 at eight per cent interest.[11] Hannig also transferred title to 78-4/10 acres of land two miles northwest from the city to O. W. Hollingsworth, who signed a promissory note for $2,250.

Hollingsworth paid $1700 in gold and $500 in silver and agreed to 18 per cent interest per annum, "payable in like coin."[12]

Hannig's furniture store on Pecan Street—between Brazos and San Jacinto—no doubt continued prosperous. The editor of a local newspaper visited the establishment in October and described it in one of his local items as "one of the largest in the state." He was especially impressed with the stock of beautiful bedroom suites and mirrors[13] Hannig had selected during his summer trip to markets in New York, Cincinnati, and Chicago.[14] Hannig took out a page one advertisement in the *Statesman* to announce a sale, offering "great bargains" at "bottom prices" on furniture of all types, carpets, oil cloths, and matting.[15]

While the sale was in progress, Hannig deeded to Matthew Kreisle 23 feet off block 66, lot 1, fronting 23 feet on Pecan and running back 128 feet. Kreisle paid $7,000 for the property.[16]

On Oct. 18, 1874, John Cardwell published an ebullient item about Hannig's store, and one can assume that the gift desk resulted in this publicity:

A NEW DESK—This local is happy, he is proud, for he now writes on an elegant new $25 desk from that extensive establishment of J. W. Hannig. Style and convenience is all the rage in these modern times, and we have to keep up with the balance of mankind. All those that want to be happy should go to Hannig's and get new furniture.

An astute businessman, Hannig widened his circle of influential friends through Knights Templar, Masonic, and the Washington Fire Engine Company organizations and through community affairs. A number of merchants—Hannig among them—met in the mayor's office Tuesday, Oct. 27, to organize a Board of Trade. Hannig accepted appointment to a committee to draw up by-laws, serving with Walter Tips, C. A. Koechler, W. B. Smith, John Bremond, and B. R. Bonner. William Brueggerhoff presided over the organizational session, probably resorting frequently to his gavel to break into the whispering. The businessmen were excited over a fire which that very afternoon had consumed the roof of Ben Thompson's drug store.

Authorities were suggesting that arson had been a part of the picture. A rock in the basement of the frame building behind the Avenue Hotel had been removed and fire put underneath the floor.[17]

Hannig and approximately 100 businessmen of Austin accepted an invitation of B. R. Bonner to tour the Austin City Mills 3 p.m., Nov. 24, and then to enjoy a "bountiful repast." While Hannig was thus occupied, Susanna gave thought to her Christmas fruit cake. A. S. Roberts was offering three pounds of almonds for $1, citron was priced at 60 cents a pound, and six pounds of currants were going for $1.

When he returned from the Mill tour, Hannig gave his wife a detailed account of the plant. Bonner had told Austin merchants how he had taken over the establishment, which was producing a medium quality of flour. He vowed he would advance the grades of flour as the market required, but almost immediately women in the area called for "a quality equal to the best imported brands." Bonner had responded.

"If there is eloquence, beauty and convincing power in anything," he had told the men, "I now present it in the following cheerful and irresistible testimony, given by many of Austin's fairest and most accomplished ladies, to the superior quality of flour manufactured by Austin's City Mills."

Bonner then read testimonials by a number of prominent Austin women—Mrs. A. B. Palm, Mrs. Lucinda Raymond, Mrs. E. J. Davis, Mrs. Lilly Graham, and Mrs. James H. Raymond.

And he quoted Mrs. J. W. Hannig as having said, "I have used your XXXX Rising Star flour in loaf bread and biscuits and like it as well as any flour I have ever used. I hope it will receive the patronage it so richly deserves."

Not enthusiastic—Hannig probably reflected after Bonner had read the statement—but exactly what Susanna said about the product.

The smell of cedar, not yet taken down after the holidays, was beginning to permeate the entire house with its fragrance, and the sounds of Christmas lingered delightfully in their minds when Susanna and J. W. went to bed Dec. 28. Hannig was aroused from sleep when a niece screamed. Hannig ran to the girl's room in time to see a figure jump through the window. Hannig rushed for his pistol but fell over a chair.

After calming the child, Susanna and Hannig began an inventory of their home. Susanna was certain $5 had been taken from her portfolio, and Hannig concluded that his pockets had been rifled of $4.75.

For days, neighbors and friends of the Hannigs talked of little but the robbery. There had been a rash of thievery. A young man had been caught in Ben Hendrick's cellar, and his weak alibi—that he was looking for a woman—could leave no doubt that he had been caught in a robbery. Dr. S. W. Baker had lost a sidesaddle and a set of harness valued at $20. Mr. Whitcut had lost a set of harness for which he had paid $18, and Seiders was missing some harness of the same value. Three saddles had been lifted from William Smyth's place.[18]

After such an eventful end to the old year, the Hannigs faced 1875 with hope. So did other Austinites. A contract had been signed for a wooden toll bridge across the Colorado, and it had been estimated that between $80,000 and $200,000 would be required to improve the approaches to the bridge. While some citizens talked about the progress—the fact that the community was becoming a city—little did they dream that before long, a herd of cattle would bring the downfall of that very bridge. As the herd approached the first span, the cattle began milling, reluctant to step on the boards. Their weight caused the timbers to split and give way, dumping the entire herd into the river 50 feet below. Only a few head of cattle emerged from the Colorado waters.[19]

Despite hopes for an expanding business, late in the spring, Hannig announced that he was taking a partner, Matthew Kreisle of Goliad, who would associate with the furniture store July 1. Hannig did not, however, give up his undertaking business.

In 1877 William Brueggerhoff, deciding that the city fathers would never get around to laying drainage pipe, built his own sewer down the alley east of Congress. The sewer carried the water to the river.[20] And frequently passengers on the streetcar had to step from the car to help push that vehicle, normally powered by a team of mules.[21]

The year, women would remember, was when green grape pies were fashionable and when butter was 15 cents a pound, eggs were selling for 11 cents a dozen if your own flock failed to meet your needs. Potatoes were $1.10 a bushel, and onions reeked in the markets at $6 a barrel.[22]

For the Hannig-Kreisle Store, 1877 was the year of the big auction. An advertisement on the front page of the *Statesman* notified citizens what they could expect—bargains in all types of furniture—if they attended the auction, beginning 10 a.m. Saturday, Sept. 29, and continuing "day-to-day until the entire stock is sold."[23]

Hannig's undertaking business also thrived, and in March, 1878, he ordered two new hearses, an act he dutifully reported to his friend, publisher John Cardwell. Cardwell chronicled the matter in the pages of his *Statesman*:

> One of them is said to be the finest ever brought to the State, and next best to any manufactured in the United States. The other is a child's hearse, beautiful in pattern and snow white.

Hannig kept the old hearses but made it clear that they would be considered "second class" in the future. The new ones would be stabled at Miller's and could be ordered at any time. Hannig announced arrangements to have a man sleep at his store every night as a convenience for his customers.[24]

When these hearses were delivered, the first of May, the journalist boasted that the $3,000 vehicles were "models of beauty and are of the latest improvements."[25]

In preparation for spring, Hannig added a "nice new awning" to his building, 207 Pecan, in February, 1879.[26] The structure, which brick masons had designed with cornices of "variety and dignity."[27] was filled with "a large stock of metallic cases, coffins, robes, etc. No finer in the state."[28]

An advertisement in the *Statesman* Nov. 16, 1879, informed readers that Hannig had sold his undertaking establishment:

Monroe Miller

Has Purchased the Undertaking Business

of

J. W. Hanning [sic]

And will conducted [sic] the same in connection with the

well known

ECLIPSE STABLE

And is prepared to furnish
Metallic cases and caskets
Walnut and rosewood coffins
Burial robes, etc.
On short notice.
Teams, Hearses & Carriages

Always to Order.

Orders can be left at Eclipse Stable

Any hour, day or night.[29]

The page that carried the two-column advertisement announcing the sale also contained a statement in the news columns.

Having sold my entire business to Mr. Monroe Miller, on retiring I wish to express my sincere thanks to numerous customers, and recommend my successor as a prompt and energetic business man worthy of their patronage, and who

is prepared to furnish everything pertaining to the undertaking business.

Respectfully,
J. W. Hannig.

Appearing on the same page was an advertisement for Kreisle's
furniture store and for his undertaking enterprise. ''Mr. Kreisle
gives his personal attention to all orders in the undertaking hue.
He has the finest hearses . . . .''

Not one to remain idle long, Joseph W. Hannig soon held
controlling interest in the Colorado Mills and was predicting that
before long the mill would be running night and day ''and, with
never ceasing toil, it will undoubtedly be of vast benefit to the
community.'' And the editor of the *Statesman* agreed, saying,
''When Mr. H. takes hold of anything he does so in earnest. He
has proven himself a success in trade in Austin for near a quarter
of a century, and we are glad to know that he has now put money
in this enterprize, that can be made most profitable when properly
conducted.''[30]

Originally known as the Chambers Mill, the enterprise was
located below the city a mile, where a 708 foot long seven foot-
high dam had been built across the river, backing water ''nearly
up to East Avenue'' and thus forming a beautiful lake. When
Hannig made his first inspection in February, the mill house was
four and a half stories high and the owners were predicting the
structure soon would be ready for milling.[31]

Intent on using all technical advances to the mill's ad-
vantage, Hannig became interested in a new gadget. ''By turning
a crank, any house or person renting a station may have his wire
switched to any of the other stations, and have direct communication with the station.'' It was this explanation which interested Hannig. The telephone company announced the in-
stallation of the first phones in Austin in midsummer, 1880. Supplies for the first set of stations left Chicago the first week of the
month and were due in Austin. Poles, thirty feet high, were
scheduled for delivery to be installed along Congress Avenue.
The city had approved construction of the ''line in the streets of
the city.''

Monroe Miller, who had purchased the undertaking business from Hannig and ran it in connection with his Eclipse Stable, took the first station, and the wires were strung into his office July 19. Among the first five placing orders for stations were J. W. Hannig for Colorado Flour and Col. Hoxie for the International Depot.

Control of the switchboard was located in Jones Library Hall. Stations, consisting of a bell telephone, Blake transmitter, and bell magneto call box, were available for a monthly rental fee from $55 to $60.[32]

Not all went well for Hannig, however, and the personal and local column of the Austin *Statesman*, on Sunday, Nov. 14, 1880, reported that he had lost "a pair of very fine mules," for which he had paid $500. Cause of death was unknown.

CHAPTER SEVEN

AUSTIN

IN the early 1870's, the Hannigs resided on Pine Street, between Neches and Red River,[1] but before the decade began its downhill run, Susanna and Joseph W. Hannig built a two-story frame home on the northeast city limits, on Duval and 32nd Street. The house crowned a high piece of ground, beyond which stretched the favorite barbecue and picnic site of young Austinites. Not far away, on the banks of Waller Creek, was a community of blacks—among whom was an elderly man who claimed that he had been Susanna's slave prior to the Emancipation Proclamation.[2]

How pleasant the new surroundings must have been for Susanna. The peach orchard she and J. W. planted became recognized as one of the finest in central Texas,[3] and she took pride in her garden. Her kitchen must have reeked when Susanna prepared her favorite meal—cornbread, cabbage, bacon, and buttermilk.[4]

The house frequently resounded with young persons—three of her grandchildren[5] and the nieces and nephews by marriage. E. A. Masur, pioneer merchant of Lockhart, recalled visiting frequently. Of his aunt, he wrote:

She was a very dignified old lady and all who knew her respected her, and she was always ready to talk about her past experiences, but I was too young, to my regret in later life, to take much interest in what she had to say in those days . . . . And, too, I remember dreading, on our visits, being kissed by an old lady with hair on her upper lip.[6]

Annie Hannig, also of Lockhart, remembered Susanna as a large[7] comatula, and the ambrotype and several photographs of her suggest that on long stretches of time her blue eyes must have looked into a mirror, while she made certain that her black hair was well dressed, that her breast pin[8] was properly positioned, that the black shawl looked well with the puffy sleeves of her dress.[9]

While a majority of Austin businessmen were heading toward home at 5 p.m., March 9, 1875, several were lighting their cigars or taking seats in the Swenson Building office of Attorneys J. W. Terrell and A. S. Walker. Discussion turned to ways of improving the relationship between the city and the legislature. What these men decided probably sent Austin women into the millinery and dry goods stores the next day. A ball and supper on Friday, March 12.

Several committees were appointed before the men adjourned, and named to the reception committee with J. W. Hannig were Representative A. W. Terrell, Judge Z. T. Fulmore, A. P. Wooldridge, V. C. Giles, A. J. Peeler, Editor John Cardwell, A. H. Robinson, Fire Chief J. A. Nagle, and A. S. Mair.

Like many of her neighbors and friends, as soon as her husband came through the door with the news, Susanna probably began thinking of her wardrobe requirements. Would her tan, faille silk gown with bowknots and brown drapery be suitable?[10] Or, she might wear her violet Irish poplin dress with the three folds of violet velvet. The tunic was looped at each side with a velvet rosette and trimmed with silk fringe. And her long strand of jet beads would make it an appropriate costume.[11] She may have visited Friedberger & Bros.' Temple of Fashion early the next day, for here a special sale in progress included Irish poplins and silk at 40 cents a yard, two- or three-button gloves, ladies silk neckties, and white hose.[12] She probably hesitated over counters of specials—turkey red table damask at 80 to 85 cents, ladies cloth shoes, taffeta ribbons, or hemstitched handkerchiefs at 25 cents each.[13]

When the ladies and their escorts stepped from their rented landaus to enter the doors of the Raymond House on the evening of March 12, they could hear the 10-piece orchestra under the baton of George Herzog. Several couples, recovering from their surprise at seeing the dancing area ablaze with gas lights, found the violins too inviting, and they soon were dancing the gavotte. Austin citizens, state officials, legislators and their escorts—formally attired for an evening of gaiety—soon were gliding across the floor.

"Aye, Mr. Speaker," a legislator jested from the dance area.

"I am not the Speaker," answered a beautiful young blonde to whom the address had been directed.

"I intend to have you substituted for Mr. Bryan,"[14] the legislator said before a broad grin spread over his flushed face.

"Very well," continued the woman. "I am big enough to wear his . . . clothes."

Those dancers close enough to overhear the final word of the conversation laughed, and the young woman, obviously embarrassed, made it clear that she was heading for the room where food was being served. Before long, others had joined her and Professor Herzog called for a respite for his musicians. The military brass band struck up "The Maid of Monterrey," playing from the balcony of the patio. Soon guests had filed from the dance floor onto the courtyard, a space measuring 100 by 20 feet which, for the evening, had been covered with canvas. Tables from the dining room of the hotel had been moved and were now forming two long tables accommodating 200 guests.

Guests entering the patio were impressed with the tables, pristine white under their cloths, and literally groaning under the load of food—800 pounds of corn fed beef, "nice fat deer," several roast pigs, "nice fat turkeys and chickens" prepared in butter and herbs, oyster soup, rich jellies, and sauces. And after platters of these foods had been removed, white-frocked waiters set on the tables silver stands of white cakes, decorated with pink roses, and compotes of nuts, candies, and fruit—Havana oranges, Catawba grapes, figs, and raisins—and before each guest they placed dishes of chocolate and vanilla ice cream, a delicacy comparatively new to Austin and still regarded as a chic dessert.

Several times during the evening, persons directed questions to Susanna about the law passed late the afternoon before—a law that would exempt the old Alamo Church from taxation. And there was talk about the Senate's bill to pay Capt. L. H. McNelly and his company of Texas Rangers for their work in the Sutton-Taylor feud in DeWitt County.[15]

And talk about Representative Davis's resolution drew smiles. "And the House passed it," said one diner.

"What does it do?"

"Limit to five minutes the time each legislator could talk on the floor . . . ."

". . . on the same subject."

After the gorged guests had finished their ice cream, special dignitaries were introduced—Governor Richard Coke, an aristocratic man who had not outgrown his Virginia heritage; Lieutenant Governor Richard B. Hubbard with his head of thick brown hair and his face covered with a brown beard and moustache; and other state officials.[16]

No doubt, as the guests waited in front of the Raymond House for their carriages to arrive from Miller's Eclipse Stable, they congratulated Manager George W. Honey, proprietor, on his "newly refitted" house, on the food, and on the service.[17] No doubt, too, such tunes as "Darling Nellie Gray," "Juanita," and "Listen to the Mocking Bird" were fresh in their minds.

His duties on the reception committee for the dinner and ball completed, J. W. Hannig turned his attention to matters of business. On June 27, he signed a deed for a residence on Willow Street. The house, he reasoned, would be well worth the $1800 asking price, for it was between the Colorado River and the expanding community—ideal rent property.

The summer—although hot and humid—proved a pleasant one for the Hannig family. On July 24, 1875, twelve Austinites received a letter. Addressed were lawyer W. M. Walton, editor John Cardwell, George B. Zimpelman, F. Everett, B. Melasky, W. H. Tobin the druggist, Louis Maas, Ed Creary, Jacob Stern, J. D. Logan, publisher John D. Elliott, and Hannig. The letter read:

Gentlemen:
The spontaneous burst of sentiment throughout the State to provide a home for Jefferson Davis and the unanimity and concord that has followed this proposition, has induced the undersigned—being moved to aid in the accomplishment of this laudable desire to give two brilliant dramatic entertainments at the Opera House during the coming week, the proceeds of which, except for the actual expenses incident to carrying out of this purpose, shall be set aside for the end and aim in view; and in order to evince the fullest fidelity and insure the largest practical result. You are hereby requested to act as a committee to supervise the entertainment in question and to receive the money at the door.
We have the honor to be your obedient servants.
J. A. Baughn
William Edings,
Lessees and Managers.

On the day that copies of the letter were received, Hannig and his associates met, agreed to accept the responsibility, suggested that Ben Honnet and Seraph Melasky act as a committee for ticket sales, and wrote the Opera House managers.

They said:
We will take pleasure in co-operating with you in this laudable undertaking and will immediately take steps to successfully accomplish it . . . .

One of the committee members approached John Cardwell, editor of the *Statesman*, who saw that both pieces of correspondence appeared in his newspaper along with a story announcing that the romantic drama, ''Kathleen Mavournean,'' would be performed. Managers of the Opera House promised that the play, popular for many years, would be ''produced with every attention to detail, new scenery, costumes, and appointments,'' and would be followed by a series of tableaux illustrating the song, ''Officer's Funeral.'' In answer to special requests, ''Nan, the Good-for-Nothing,'' a ''laughable farce''[18] with Nattie Saphore as the irrepressible Nan, was added to the theatre fare.[19]

When Wednesday, July 28, was announced as the date for the first benefit, members of the committee began pushing the sale of tickets. Their ladies began to discuss whether they would wear tulle, lace, or foulard. Did they need new kid gloves or were they too hot for this time of year? Would their garnet necklace go with the pale blue dress? Susanna may have reminded herself since laundering it that she had not rebasted the cotton dust ruffle in her verdigris princess dress she planned to wear.[20] Her gold lace fan would complement the dress.[21]

To encourage Austinites to attend the production, members of the committee submitted a story to the newspaper, calling attention to the fact that several young ladies would be present to wait upon the audience with ice cream and sherbets prepared by Mr. O'Neal, the proceeds to go to the Jefferson Davis fund.[22] Certainly those members of the committee who had seen the Irish drama called attention of prospective ticket buyers that the production contained not one but several numbers including the ballad that perpetuates the play's name.[23]

As residents talked in the lobby of the Opera House, Wednesday night, they asked for any new word on the contractor Beckway. He had been putting an addition to Smith's store on Pecan Street. Beckway had disappeared Saturday evening after settling accounts with his hands but not with the lumber dealers.

''The editor of the *Statesman* said he thought the case one of intentional wrong to his creditors. Think so?''

And others chatted about the steamer *Sunbeam* which had plied the Colorado River with a party of excursionists. And still others mentioned A. S. Roberts's advertisements offering dried buffalo meat for ten cents a pound. "Delicious for chipping" read the notice.[24]

No doubt Susanna and other wives of committee members listened with patience as their husbands expressed disappointment over the turn out. "Very good," but "not so good as it was expected that occasion would bring," said one of the workers. And some found fault with the amusements writer for the *Statesman*, who mentioned in a two-line review that the comedietta[25] "Nan the Good-for-Nothing" brought down the house at the theatre. Nothing was written about the acting in "Kathleen Mavournean," which had been promoted as "the most beautiful and touching drama ever presented."[26] Yet, the critic did mention the fine effects and the beautiful tableaux. The reviewer, instead, discussed that a picture of Jefferson Davis hung in a conspicuous place in the Opera House hall and that evergreen garlands had been draped throughout the building. Several women of the community presided over a table where ice cream and cake were served.[27]

A second benefit was held July 31, and in what may have been an attempt to make amends for the slight publicity, the *Statesman* editor mentioned that following the performance, the Opera House would be closed a month—until the company could be strengthened with new actors and new scenery added and old sets rejuvenated. Journalist Cardwell reminded Austinites that when Jefferson Davis had visited the city in May "thousands flocked to the streets and about his hotel to see him and do him honor, and we regret that a more general response has not met the efforts of the theatre company to give him a benefit."[28]

A number of Austinites attending the theatre the second night of the benefit could recall waiting at the train station for the arrival of Jefferson Davis that day in May. A newspaper writer had called the group the largest crowd ever assembled at the depot on any occasion. Only shortly before the scheduled hour, words were whispered that the train would be late. And it was, arriving at 11 a.m., not 8:40. But when the old president of the Confederacy stepped off the platform, he was led over the muddy Congress Avenue in a parade. The Travis Rifles in blue, cadets of the Military Institute in gray, Herzog's brass band and civilians joined the procession. Jeff Davis, Gov. Coke, Ex-Governor Francis Lubbock, and Mayor Wheeler in a fine landau rented for the occasion led the procession up Pecan Street to the Avenue and to a stop at the Avenue Hotel.[29]

That evening, when Susanna and J. W. and their friends gathered in the theatre foyer, they talked of the thief who ten days earlier had taken a saddle horse from Murchison's, the stable under this very Opera House building.

"Editor Cardwell says the man just 'forgot to return' the animal."

"Now that he's been caught in San Antonio, he'll pay for that absentmindedness. He'll be returned to Austin for trial."

For many Austin women, whose life tended toward routine, shelling black-eyed peas on the porch and chatting with neighbors who shared the task, taking the buggy for a drive to the barbecue grounds, fingering the muslin in Friedberger's Temple of Fashion, or pruning the wisteria as soon as its lavendar clusters had fallen could mean excitement. A letter asking permission to visit might be like a ticket to adventure, but not to Susanna, to whom a visit might be a ticket to reviving memories. Such was the occasion on Sept. 23, 1876, when she agreed to talk with an out-of-state writer. That guest recorded:

Called on Mrs. Susanna Hannig, whose husband Joseph Hannig is living with her. She was at the sacking of the Alamo in 1836, 6th March; was then in her 15th year; was then named Susannah Dickerson, wife of Lieut. Almarion Dickerson, and her maiden name was Susanna Wilkerson. Her parents were in Williamson Co., Tenn. Her husband was one of the killed. They had one child, a daughter, who, then an infant was with them in the Alamo; this daughter married John Maynard Griffith, a native of Montgomery Co., Texas, by whom she had 4 children, all 4 of whom are living. She died in Montgomery Co., Texas about the year 1871.

The Mexicans came unexpectedly into San Antonio & her husband & child retreated into the Fort. Enemy began throwing bombs into Fort, but no one hurt till the last day, i.e., The assault except one horse killed. Had provisions enough to last the besieged 30 days.

Among the besieged were 50 or 60 wounded men from Cos's fight. About 18 cannon (she believes) were mounted on parapet & in service at all times. The enemy gradually approached by means of earth works thrown up. Besieged were looking for reinforcements which never arrived. The only outsiders who succeeded in coming into Fort were 3 of our spys who entered 3 days before the assault & were all killed.

Dr. Horace Alsbury (bro. of Perry Alsbury of San Antonio) retreated into the Fort for protection with his Mexican wife & sister-in-law. He left, unknown to witness, & the two women escaped to the enemy & betrayed our situation about 2 days before the assault.

On morning of 6th March, about daylight enemy threw up signal rocket & advanced & were repulsed. They rallied & made 2nd assault with scaling ladders, first thrown up on E side of Fort. Terrible fight ensued. Witness retired into a room of the old Church & saw no part of fight—Though she could distinctly hear it. After the fall she was approached by a Col. Black (an Englishman) and officer in the Mexican service, who sheltered her from Mexican injury & took her in a buggy to Mr. Musquiz, a merchant in town, where she staid till next day when she was conducted before Santa Anna who threatened to take her to Mexico with her child; when Almonte, his nephew, addressing his English, pleaded for witness, saying he had been in N. O. & had experienced great kindness from Americans. Witness was then permitted to depart to her home in Gonzales. Col. Travis commanded the Fort. A Negro man named Joe, was in the Fort, & was the slave & body servant of Col. Travis. After the fall of the Alamo, Joe was forced by the Mexicans at the point of the bayonet, to point out to them the bodies of Col. Travis & Col. Crockett among the heaps of dead. Joe was the only negro in the Fort. Witness infant was the only child in the fort. The witness & the two Mexican women already mentioned were the only women in the fort.

The witness has had no children in her present marriage.

On April 4, 1876, a distinguished lawyer arrived from Arkansas. To some Texans, he was a "chip off the old block"—much like his famous grandfather, Davy Crockett. Robert H. Crockett visited with Mrs. Hannig, no doubt, discussing the Alamo and the parts that their dear ones had played in the battle, and also discussing plans for the American Centennial Year. Crockett was enthusiastic about his plans to visit Philadelphia, and he intended to take with him the rifle that Philadelphia citizens had presented his grandfather 41 years earlier, a watch that had belonged to Davy, and an original portrait of the hero.

Mrs. Hannig also was making arrangements to attend the Centennial celebration, probably making the trip with her husband as he visited the markets.[30]

Little did John Cardwell, editor of the *Statesman*, realize that the item he published in his column April 7, 1877, would be like the first bead on a strand. It was a lazy news day; he had space to fill. As he pondered what to run, he doodled, then in a clear longhand, suitable to send to the printer, he wrote:

There are several old soldiers of the Texas revolution in Austin and in adjacent towns and counties and these should meet on the twenty-first instant—San Jacinto Day. Two years ago the old colored body servant of Col. Travis[31] was in this city and his home was not far away. Why not have him brought to the capital? The only white survivor of the Alamo is here, and we do not see why the veterans should not be *feted* by the city government or by the citizens of the capital.[32]

Cardwell glanced over the item before sending it to the backshop. Not bad, he mused. Has a local angle—Susanna Hannig. Has a future look with San Jacinto Day only two weeks away. Not bad at all.

City fathers apparently paid little heed to the journalist, and San Jacinto Day passed with little in the way of celebration. The members of the fire department did hold a picnic, but the traditional speeches and gathering of veterans were overlooked.[33]

On March 14, 1878, Charles W. Evers, editor of the *Wood County Sentinel* of Ohio was making a tour of Texas when he stopped in Austin. An interview with Susanna was arranged, and Evers wrote an account of his visit with the heroine of the Alamo:

> . . . For one of the most pleasing incidents of my stay in Austin I am indebted to Col. Dupre, editor of the Austin Statesman, who kindly drove out with me two miles on a short visit to one of the most historic and to me interesting women of today. I refer to Mrs. Dickinson, now Mrs. J. W. Hannig, the only white survivor of the Alamo massacre, over forty years ago. We were made welcome at her beautiful home, which is on one of those commanding locations for which Austin is noted, overlooking the city and surrounding country . . . .
>
> Mrs. Hannig is an intelligent woman of excellent memory, and is perhaps not far from 60 years of age, although but few grey hairs are yet noticeable on her head. She engaged readily in conversation about that dark episode in her history which robbed her of her husband and partially of her reason for a time. As she conversed she seemed at times to stop as if in a sudden reverie or dream, and I fancied I saw almost a wild light dancing in her eyes for a moment, and it would not be strange, for her recital of the events of that awful day will excite the most stolid listener. If Mrs. Hannig was so inclined or if her circumstances required it (happily they do not) she could go on the lecture platform and draw crowded houses in any city in the United States.[34]

To Evers, Susanna also mentioned that she would like to see the play, ''Davy Crockett,'' then on the boards of some opera houses.

Almost a year after Cardwell had suggested that the two survivors of the Alamo arrange a meeting in Austin, once again groping to fill his column, the journalist focused attention on Mrs. Hannig. He had been reading Reuben Potter's pamphlet on the Alamo, the content of which had appeared originally in the *North American Review*, and had noticed the differences between accounts by Mrs. Hannig, an eyewitness to the siege, and those recited by Potter, acclaimed as an authority on the subject. So, Cardwell asked in his personal column in the *Statesman*:

> Why doesn't Frank Mayo come into Texas with his properly organized company and play "Davy Crockett?" Moreover, Mr. Mayo should visit Austin and learn from the lips of the only living American who was in the Alamo when the massacre occurred, a share of truth affecting the horrible event.[35]

Was the editor playing promotion agent? Had he been fed advanced information by Add Smith, owner of the Opera House, that Frank Mayo would appear in "Davy Crockett" in March?

Not many days passed before the Texas-sized posters informed Austinites that Frank Mayo would indeed appear in the Texas capital. With a troupe of a dozen actors, Mayo opened in "Davy Crockett" Friday, March 1, 1878, playing to "the most crowded audience ever gathered in the Opera House."[36] Like one local critic, Austin citizens generally considered the character of Davy Crockett "admirably sustained" by an actor with a "powerful, manly figure" and a "brave, honest face."[37]

No doubt, Susanna Hannig thought of the 28-foot posters as she dressed for the theatre, attending as a special guest of the star.[38] Her host, Mayo, had appeared before his first stage lights in San Francisco in 1856 and for 16 years received few exciting notices.[39] True, during some of his earlier performances in Nevada, he had been called one of the most promising young tragedians of the day,[40] but Mayo first drew serious attention when he was in Niblo's Garden in New York in 1874. From that time on, Frank Mayo was "Davy Crockett" in the theatrical world.[41] He was "an American Lochinvar—who because he is brave, strong and capable of sacrifice, wins the deep love of a young woman much his superior in station and education."[42]

Frank H. Murdoch's play about "Davy Crockett" drew laudatory praise; Lawrence Hutton, on the staff of the *New York Mail*, called it "among the best American plays ever written,"[43] and the reviewer for *Spirit of the Times* observed that the five-act play was "admirably constructed." He wrote:

> It is not sensational, and depends upon no clap-trap effects for favor. It fairly brims over with humanity, and appeals strongly to the hearts of all classes. Stories of the affections are ever popular with theatre-goers. Whether it be the love of the helmeted knight or the love of the rough but honest backwoodsman, like Davy Crockett, the interest is the same . . . . The element which gives "Davy Crockett" its claim to success is a simple story of pure love that runs through the play like a thread of gold. It is the poem of young Lochinvar dramatized and Americanized.[44]

No wonder there was excitement as Susanna Hannig and members of her family dressed for the theatre. And like other Austinites, they probably took deep breaths as the curtain opened on an exterior scene of Crockett's home, where a group of travelers has stopped—Major Royston, suffering from a sprained ankle; his ward, Eleanor Vaughn; her fiancé, Crampton. As soon as Eleanor sees Crockett, she recognizes a childhood friend; her love swells. Crampton seems to exert a spell over Major Royston, so when the party prepares to depart, Crockett determines to follow to protect his childhood acquaintance.

When the curtain came down, members of the family pelted Susanna with questions. Was Frank Mayo's portrayal true to Davy Crockett as she remembered him? Did Crockett ever talk about his home? Did Crockett dress that way? Did he talk that way?

It seemed that before Susanna could collect her thoughts and answer the questions, it was time for Act II. The Texans hurried to their seats; they sat hushed like a room of school boys and girls. The second act is set in Crockett's hunting lodge. A snow storm is raging. Crockett thinks about the beautiful woman who has stirred such warmth in his heart. Crampton interrupts Crockett's reverie to tell him that Eleanor is outside—lost. Davy throws open the door and rushes into the blowing snow, and before long, he drags the limp body of Eleanor into the lodge. When Eleanor revives, she is aware that her love for the back-woodsman is mutual. Davy brings out a book that Eleanor had left at his house years earlier. She opens it and reads Sir Walter Scott's Young Lockinvar legend. Meanwhile, Eleanor's betrothed snores in front of the blazing fire.

Young women in the audience sighed as the curtain closed on Act II. Weren't the lines beautiful? And who did the staging? They learned that the sets and props had been hauled into the Opera House by the troupe of players and that Vincent de Banernfeind had been in charge of them. Talk was that the man had taken a job with Add Smith and would repair the old sets in the Opera House. His brush could do a great deal to reviving the tired drops.[45]

Howling wolves surround the hunting lodge, so Davy hunts for the bar for use in securing the door. Finding that the bar has been burned, the frontiersman relies on brute strength to keep the wolves outside. Crockett is at this post as the curtain rises on the third act. Almost exhausted, he hears shouts and the firing of guns, signaling that Major Royston and Crampton have returned. Just in the nick of time. Although his arm pains him, Crockett sets off for the nearest settlement, ten miles away.

For Act IV, stagehands created the drawing room of Major Royston's house, and Texans learned through some of the dialogue that Crampton possesses several notes Royston forged under financial duress. Crampton forces the Major to agree that his ward will marry so that he might control the fortune. As the hour of that betrothal approaches, Davy Crockett enters to tell Eleanor that although he loves her, he must bid farewell. Crockett, behind a chair, learns that Eleanor is unhappy over the wedding plans and aloud she calls for a friend. Davy appears. Eleanor throws herself into his arms.

Eleanor and Davy are married in his home while her friends beg admittance. Crampton, of course, produces the forged papers but Eleanor agrees to stand good for them. Eleanor vows that she belongs by the side of Davy Crockett.[46]

"Perfectly acted," commented one of the theatregoers.

"Needs a little more roughness, a little less refinement," suggested a man.

"An idyll of the backwoods . . . ."[47]

"But how much of it is legend? How much is truth?"

"I don't know, but I liked the character as Mayo made him talk and act."[48]

"No one will ever want to see Frank Mayo play anything but Davy Crockett," said one playgoer.

One of the men in the audience could not keep from thinking of what Frank Mayo himself had once said, ". . . Damn it, when I first produced it they called it a bad dramatization of a half-dime novel. Now it's 'an idyll of the backwoods.' And now damn 'em, they call it a classic."[49]

Austinites gave him "ear-splitting applause" and the "uproar" remained "furious and continuous." Mayo stepped before the curtain and in a manner which caused the editor of the *Statesman* to label him an orator as well as an actor, the star read an item from an Austin newspaper. He said his fame was so well established that it could not be impaired by the assault for personal reasons made by a local newspaper.[50] Austin residents agreed, and they stamped their feet, yelled, and clapped approval of Frank Mayo.

While the audience cheered, Frank Mayo, his co-star, Miss Laurens, and other members of the theatrical troupe rushed from the theatre to catch the train, which had been held until 11:40 p.m. so the actors could carry the production to Brenham.[51] As the train puffed from the station, Mrs. Hannig, in a carriage heading for her home, probably recalled to members of her family how Crockett was addicted to the fiddle and how he swore long and hard when he was shut up in the enclosure of the Alamo.[52] The picture of him in the capitol, she said, was an excellent likeness.

No trip to the center of town—the capitol—was without the agony of having Alamo memories returning. There, in the foyer of the most imposing building in the community, was a monument to the heroes of the Alamo—to those men who had died around her. Susanna could not see the ten-foot high monument without thinking of Travis, Bowie, and Crockett, and of her own first husband, Almeron Dickinson. She could not read the inscription, "To the God of the Fearless and Free Is Dedicated This Altar" without hearing once again the groans of men in death. "Let the Stones of the Alamo Speak, That Their Immolation Be Not Forgotten," was the inscription on one side of the monument base, and Susanna wondered if the stone cutter knew how the stones roared to her. The Roman altar from which rose the pyramid, topped with its flame, was decorated with cannon balls and other relics scraped from the Alamo grounds, and Susanna could not see the items without wondering if they had been responsible for the death of some of the men she knew. And the spire with its torch, the symbol of freedom. How could she get her freedom from the memories that plagued her daily? And the inscription, "Thermopylae had her messenger of defeat; the Alamo had none." Susanna probably shook her head at the message. What had she been but a messenger—the one survivor charged with delivering the message that the Alamo had fallen, that it had been washed in blood?[33]

Forget the Alamo? How could she among all Texans?

CHAPTER EIGHT

THE ALAMO REMEMBERED

THE Alamo, for a second time, seemed doomed. Santa Anna had stripped the mission-fortress ''of everything not imbedded in the earth and blew apart walls and quarters not already smashed,'' leaving the Alamo gutted and in ruins. The Congress of the Republic of Texas granted the pile of rubble and surrounding property to the Roman Catholic Church. Unable to restore the building or rehabilitate the grounds, the Church leased both to the United States Army in 1847, and the Quartermaster Corps stacked saddles, tobacco, blankets, and arms within the rancid walls. In 1876, when the Quartermaster shuttled men and material to new facilities at Fort Sam Houston, the Alamo again was deserted. The following year, all the grounds except the chapel itself and the land to the south were sold to Honore Grenet for $20,000. The Frenchman erected a pair of wooden bastions, one on each side of the old Indian quarters, and placed painted cannon on what he decided were strategic positions on the room.[1]

Visitors to the Alamo became indignant at what had happened to the shrine, part of which was a warehouse and part a saloon. One woman, looking in the old chapel, had stumbled over ''bags of salt and cans of kerosene.''

''This takes all the romance out of the Alamo,'' she complained.

An elderly man, who as a child had perched on Davy Crockett's knee, could not find the spot where his hero had fallen—the mounds of canned tomatoes and dried apricots were too high.[2]

Another visitor, stepping "into the vault-like chamber—the chapel of the old Alamo mission," sat "on a beer-keg and allowed my mind to wander back into the past." A guide conducted him through the building and here is his account:

"Do you see that angle in the wall, where those old cabbages and those boxes of Limberger cheese are piled? Right there at least forty Mexicans were killed. Phew, how they smell! Reckon those Limbergers must have soured! I wonder why we can't raise them right here, instead of having to import them from the north."

"What, Mexicans?"

"No, I mean cabbages. In this room, where so much soap and axle-grease is stored, seventeen wounded Texans were shot. We have got a soap-factory right here in town; we don't have to send to the North for soap. 'Thermopylae had her messenger of defeat; the Alamo had none.' And it's a darned sight better article than the Yankees made, anyhow. Right here is the most sacred spot in Texas—and it would bring sixty dollars a month if it was rented out for a saloon,—around which the sacred memories of the past cluster."[3]

On Wednesday, April 27, 1881,—forty-five years after she had left the Alamo as a messenger of defeat, Susanna was back within the gray, musty walls, this time in the company of a representative of the San Antonio *Daily Express*; Mrs. Rebecca Black, the grandniece of Deaf Smith; Col. and Mrs. H. B. Andrews, vice-president of the Galveston, Harrisburg and San Antonio Railroad;[4] Bishop Quintard of Tennessee; Dean Walter Raleigh Richardson of St. Mark's;[5] and two young nieces of Susanna's.

In describing the visit, the *Express* reporter wrote:

114

Mrs. Hannig says there was no second story to the Alamo at that time—it was all one floor. She can give but little of the struggle

A LITTLE DARK ROOM

in the rear of the building. The party yesterday entered the appartment [sic] and even with a candle could scarcely see each other's faces. The old lady recognized almost every stone, however, and the arch overhead and the corners she said, with tears in her eyes, came back as vividly to memory as though her experiences of yore had been but yesterday. She showed the reporter where the couch had stood, and the window through which she peeped to see the blood of noble men seeping into the ground, and the bodies of heroes lying cold in death. It was in this room that she saw

THE LAST MAN FALL,

and he was a man named Walker, who had often fired the cannon at the enemy.[6]

After the tour, the group went to the saloon, and the Frenchman served the best in Grenet's Castle, Mumm's celebrated wine.[7]

Meanwhile, in Austin, the limestone capitol, its three stories crowned with a Monticello dome, was protected from cattle and horses by a white fence and from erosion by a brick retaining wall. "The architectural monstrosity that so long disfigured the crown of the heaven-kissing hill at the head of Congress Avenue," as one contemporary described the building, was not protected from other elements, and at noon Nov. 9, 1881, the place, "filled with many historical reminiscences and thousands of bats," was destroyed by fire.[8] A clerk decided to do something about the chill that hugged the soft yellow limestone walls. He installed a stove and inserted a section of pipe into a hole he believed would connect with a flue, The hole, however, was mere space between walls, and once a fire was lit, sparks flew between the walls and into the book collection room. Soon, the books were ablaze, sending sparks to the wooden walls in the rooms above.[9]

What happened to the Alamo monument?

A reporter for the Austin *Statesman* gave this account:

The firemen were driven from the Senate chamber by the fast increasing flames, but step by step they fought them. Some thoughtful persons tore away the iron railing around the monument, made from the ruins of the Alamo and carried off the upper portion. The pedestal was permitted to remain in position, as it was thought it could withstand the weight of anything which might fall upon it.[10]

Another version of what happened to the Alamo monument appeared in *Texas Siftings*:

The brave and chivalric colored man thus continued to save public property, being the coolest man on the grounds, except the four gentlemen, who assisted in demolishing the ten-foot high Alamo monument that stood in the vestibule. They deserve to have their names preserved in history. If we can learn their names, we shall publish them next week. They said the monument erected in the memory of the heroes who, for the freedom of Texas, gave their lives at the Texas Thermopyle [*sic*]—a monument carved out of the blood stained stones of the sacred Alamo, should not be allowed to perish. With tears in their eyes they went in search of an axe. It was an impressive sight to see these four old men come back with a long-handled axe, and while the lurid flames lighted up the scene and the Genus of history despairingly fluttered over the cherished monument, gave the obelisk a whack, and the record of historic deeds crumbled into small chunks of plaster of paris.[11]

No record was made of the reaction of Susanna when she heard that the monument had been destroyed in the fire—or during the fire—no account of whether she felt relieved that the reminder no longer would be visible or whether she felt saddened at the prospect that Texas might now let the Alamo heritage fade, just as the flames and smoke had helped wipe out the marker. Perhaps, her thoughts returned to that day, only months earlier, when she had made her own pilgrimage to the shrine. And one can wonder whether she had any idea that within two years, the state would purchase the chapel itself.[12] What was foremost in her mind, no doubt, was the wound that continued to plague her.[13]

Health began to decline for Susanna, and in mid February, 1883, J. W. Hannig was summoned from his furniture store in San Antonio. A telegram informed him that his wife was seriously ill. "We trust her illness will only prove temporary," commented the editor of the San Antonio *Express* in reporting the reason for Hannig's sudden departure.[14] His trust was ill founded, for on Sunday, Oct. 7, 1883, Susanna Hannig died from what the city sexton called hemorrhage of the bowels.[15]

Funeral services were held 11 a.m. Tuesday, Oct. 9, in the Hannig home. "Friends and acquaintances are invited without further notice," read an item in the newspaper.[16] A bereaved Hannig followed the body to Oakwood Cemetery, noticing that the funeral car turned off the central drive. To the right was the concrete mausoleum now holding the body of his old business associate, Matthew Kreisle. The four corners of the Kreisle lot had been marked with young cedar trees. The body of Susanna Hannig was borne to the top of the hill and laid to rest just at the edge of a motte of cedars. Throughout the cemetery, giant oak trees were releasing leaves, as brittle as parchment, but as golden as coins, and these were stacking against some of the white marble markers in the area of Susanna's resting place.

Joseph W. Hannig spent little time in Austin—only enough to take care of the post-funeral arrangements and to order a white marble marker, designed to show a piece of scroll, saying:

Sacred to the Memory of
Susan A.
Wife of
J. W. Hannig
Died
Oct. 7, 1883,
Aged 68 Years.

And below the scroll:

I go to prepare a place for thee

followed by this verse:

> We only know that thou has gone
> And that the same returnless tide,
> Which bore them from us still glides on,
> And we who mourn thee with it glide.

Journalists in Austin reminded Texans of Susanna's place in history:

> At Thermopylae no one escaped; in the Alamo, not a combatant in the citadel was left to tell the tale. But there did escape three non-combatants—Mrs. Dickenson, Mrs. Alsbury and Col. Travis' negro body servant.

Mrs. Hannig had lived to a good old age, and yet the scenes of that awful day in San Antonio dwelt as fresh in her mind to the day of her death, over forty-eight years afterward, as though they were but things of yesterday. Her name belongs to the history of Texas, and it is but a fitting tribute to the glorious memorial of her existence that she be honored by Texas. Some of the brave defenders of Texas sleep on the hill south of the city, overlooking the placid Colorado, but not one who died at the Alamo slumbers peacefully there. How proper it would be then that the mortal remains of this woman be deposited in the state burial ground, where in the future, Texas might honor the last resting place of the woman who cast her lot with mortal heroes, who have been promoted to immortality.[17]

After Hannig saw that the grave was suitably marked, he returned to San Antonio, where he was regarded as "one of the best known citizens."[18] A deed to Carl Mayer for 50 acres of land in exchange for $2300 was dated April 25, 1884, San Antonio, indicating that Hannig had taken up residence in the city at that time. He was married that year to Louisa Staacke. He continued to operate his furniture business until 1889. In ill health for some time, Hannig suffered a serious case of gastritis several days and expired at his home, 709 Avenue C. A past grand commander of the grand commandery of Knights

Templar and a past grand high priest of the Masonic grand chapter of Texas, he was described in the San Antonio *Express* obituary as a native of Germany who had arrived in Austin when he was 17 years of age to learn cabinet making. He left an estate valued at between $150,000 and $300,000.[19]

As he had requested, the body of Hannig was returned to Austin for burial next to Susanna.[20] The Colorado Commandery of Knights Templar met the remains at the depot in Austin and escorted them to Oakwood Cemetery,[21] where they were laid to rest in Lot 1, plot 363.

Writers[22] suggest that Susanna's and Hannig's graves "are closer than those of other couples in the cemetery." Hannig's marker is designed like a white marble tree trunk, on which are these words:

My Husband
Joseph W. Hannig
born
June 14, 1834;
died
June 6, 1890.

Not even death stilled the controversy surrounding Susanna Wilkerson Dickinson Hannig. During the 1936 Texas Centennial, marking the state's 100th year of independence from Mexico, lavender granite markers from the Hill Country were scattered throughout the state like autumn leaves. Not one honored Susanna, the "woman of the Alamo." One of the individuals who crusaded to see that the slight was corrected was E. A. Masur of Lockhart,[23] who wrote widely-read columnist Boyce House:

I knew this Lady the last ten years of her life, from 1873 'till Oct. 7th 1883, when she died. She married my Mother's brother and thereby became my Aunt. Many is the time she kissed me when, as a little boy, we would go to see them in Austin.

At the last session of the Legislature H.B. No. 483 was introduced by the Hon. J. T. Ellis, our representative from here, and strongly advicated [*sic*] by Judge Weinert[24] of Seguin, to that effect. That bill passed the lower House without a disenting [*sic*] vote but was killed in Comitee [*sic*] room in the Senate. Was ridiculed by a member of the Comitee as a GRAVE YARD BILL.[25]

On another occasion, Masur wrote House:

That the Texans were defeated at the Alamo every School Child knows and that my old Aunt was an *accredited* messenger can not be denied so that she was an historical person, whose memmory [*sic*] should be preserved to future generations for the glory of the State more than for her own glory therefore we think that she should not lie in an unmarked grave and that the State of Texas through its Legislature is the one to record the facts.

Yes, she has a credible Marble Monument at the head of her grave. It is about 8 foot high and about 16 inches square at the base. Same gives her name, as the wife of J. W. Hannig, Died, Oct. 7th, 1883. Age 68 years and a verse, but not one sylable [*sic*] about her historic past. This monument was, of course, erected by Mr. Hannig and studiously avoids doing that.[26]

We contend that the Legislature is the only one who has the right to authorize the placing [sic] of such a marker at the side of her grave. It need not be an expensive slab.[27]

For ten or twelve years, Masur carried on a campaign. At his request, Judge J. T. Ellis of Beeville, representing Hays and Caldwell Counties in the legislature, introduced a bill calling for a monument at Susanna's grave. State Senator R. A. Weinert supported the measure, but ''something always happened; it never cleared the final hurdle.'' Then, in 1947 William George Richards, representative of Lockhart, introduced the bill again; again it cleared the house but was rejected in the Senate.

Somehow, the departmental appropriation bill was passed, containing a $500 appropriation in the Parks Board budget for erection of a monument to Mrs. Susanna Dickinson Hannig at Oakwood Cemetery. Gordon K. Shearer, executive secretary of the Parks Board, announced that his group was "ready to go ahead" if someone would tell him what inscription should be included. He warned that the appropriation would lapse if the marker were not ordered before Aug. 31. If the original bill had passed, the problem would not have existed, for the measure specified "which monument shall have carved thereon the following inscription 'Mrs. Suana Dickinson Hannig, Mother of the Babe of the Alamo.'"[28]

E. A. Masur did not live to see his crusade completed. He died in 1948, and at 4 p.m., March 2, 1949, the State of Texas staged ceremonies to unveil the slab of white marble over the resting place of Susanna Hannig. The slab shows an outline of the Alamo chapel with an explanation that Mrs. Susanna Dickinson Hannig was mother of the "Babe of the Alamo." With A. Garland Adair, curator of the Texas Memorial Museum, and Mrs. Jane Y. McCallum, former secretary of state, as speakers, the marker was dedicated. Mrs. Walter Prescott Webb, Mrs. Paul Goldman, and Mrs. J. Jones from the William Travis Chapter, Mrs. W. B. Matthews from the Stephen F. Austin Chapter, and Mrs. L. V. Labenski from the Reuben Hornsby Chapter represented Daughters of the Republic of Texas at the ceremonies.[29]

❖❖❖

At 3 p.m., Saturday, March 6, 1976—between showers—a crowd of approximately fifty persons assembled in the State Cemetery, Austin, to unveil a marker honoring Susanna Dickinson Hannig. Services, conducted by the Texian Chapter of the Daughters of the Republic of Texas under the leadership of Ann Pollard Arthur, included the unveiling by A. Stasswender, who designed the monument; words by Mrs. R. E. Nitschke, Jr., great-granddaughter of Susanna Dickinson; a brief speech by Dr. C. Richard King, professor of journalism at The University of Texas; invocation by the Rev. Charles Sumners, former rector of St. David's Episcopal Church, Austin; and a message by Vicki Clark, representative for State Representative Sarah Weddington. The stone, approximately four and a half feet tall, shaped like the state, was created of Texas sunset red granite from Marble Falls; the metal marker is an outline of the Alamo Chapel.

FAMILY CHART

Susanna A. Wilkerson
1814-1883
m.
Almeron Dickinson
-1836
Angelina Elizabeth Dickinson
Dec. 14, 1834
m.
John Maynard Griffith
July 8, 1851

1. Almeron Dickinson Griffith, b. May 13, 1853, in Montgomery County, Texas; died in Austin July 13, 1938. M. Jessie Freeman Tedford.
   A. Susanna Gertrude Griffith m. Charles W. Ramsdell, two children
   B. Maude Griffith m. Ernest Griffith (a distant cousin), May 15, 1907, one child, Margaret
   C. George Maynard Griffith m. Verona Imelda Carroll, three children
   D. Alice Lucile Griffith m. Curtis McKallip, one child
   E. Jessie Angeline m. J. N. Allison, no issue
   F. Marian Willard Griffith m. Robert E. Nitschke Jr., no issue
2. Susanna Arabella, b. Jan. 13, 1855; m. Fred Sterling; died in San Antonio July 17, 1929. No issue.
3. Joseph Griffith, b. 1857 in Houston, died July 17, 1924. m. Theresa Galverira. Issue.
   A. Joseph   B. Lorraine   C. Rosalind

Second Marriage
of
Angelina Elizabeth
to
Oscar Holmes
1864

1. Sallie Holmes, b. Sept. 6, 1865, in New Orleans; m. Ben Barrera Aug. 21, 1883. Issue.
   A. Susan   B. Jodie   C. Manuel   D. George

BIBLIOGRAPHY

Adair, A. Garland. *Austin, Its Place Under Texas Skies* (Austin: Texas Information Service, 1946).

Adair, A. Garland and M. H. Crockett, Jr., editors, *Heroes of the Alamo* (New York: Exposition Press, 1957).

Adams, W. Davenport. *A Dictionary of the Drama* (London: Chatto & Windsor 1904), Vol. 1.

Allen, O. F. *The City of Houston from Wilderness to Wonder* (Temple: Privately Printed, 1936).

Anderson, John Q. *Tales of Frontier Texas, 1830-1860* (Dallas: Southern Methodist University Press, 1966).

Barkley, Mary Starr. *A History of Central Texas* (Austin: Austin Printing Company, 1970).

_____. *History of Travis County and Austin, 1839-1899* (Waco: Texian Press, 1963).

Bigelow, Maybelle S. *Fashions in History: Apparel in the Western World* (Minneapolis: Burgess Publishing Company, 1970).

Brown, John Henry. *Indian Wars and Pioneers of Texas* (Austin: L. E. Daniell, 1895).

Burke, James Wakefield. *Missions of Old Texas* (Cranbury, N. J.: A. S. Barnes and Co., 1971).

Burleson, Georgia J., editor. *The Life and Writings of Rufus Burleson* (No place given: Privately Published, 1901).

Carter, Hodding. *Doomed Road of Empire* (New York: McGraw-Hill Company, 1963).

Carrington, Evelyn M., editor. *Women in Early Texas* (Austin: Jenkins Publishing Company, 1975).

Carter, James D. *Masonry in Texas* (Waco: Committee on Education and Service for the Grand Lodge of Texas, A.F. and A.M., 1955).

Coleman, James M. *Aesculapius on the Colorado* (Austin: The Encino Press, 1971).

Daniels, A. Pat. *Texas Avenue at Main Street* (Houston: Allen Press, 1964).

Davis, Robert E., editor. *Diary of William Barret Travis* (Waco: Texian Press, 1966).

DeShields, James T. *Tall Men with Long Rifles* (San Antonio: The Naylor Company, 1971).

DeWees, William B. *Letters from an Early Settler of Texas-* (Waco: Texian Press, 1968).

Dickerson, Donna Lee. *A Typestick of Texas History* (Austin: Department of Journalism Development Fund, The University of Texas, 1972).

Freund, Max, editor. *Gustav Dresel's Houston Journal* (Austin: University of Texas Press, 1964).

Gallegly, Joseph. *Footlights on the Border* (Gravenhage: Mouton & Co., 1962).

_____. *From Alamo Plaza to Jack Harris's Saloon* (The Hague: Mouton, 1970).

Green, Rena Maverick, editor. *Memoirs of Mary A. Maverick* (San Antonio: Alamo Printing Co., 1921).

Kelley, Dayton, editor. *Texas: Her Resources and Her Public Men* (Waco: The Texian Press, 1969), originally published in Philadelphia by Ernest Crozet.

Hart, Katherine. *Waterloo Scrapbook, 1968-1970* (Austin: The Encino Press, 1970).

_____. *Waterloo Scrapbook, 1971-1972.* (Austin: The Encino Press, 1972).

Hewitt, Barnard. *Theatre, U.S.A., 1668-1957* (New York: McGraw-Hill Book Company, Inc., 1959).

History of Tennessee (Nashville: The Goodspeed Publishing Co., 1887).

Houston, American Guide Series (Houston: The Anson Jones Press, 1942).

Huston, Cleburne. *Deaf Smith: Incredible Texas Spy* (Waco: Texian Press, 1973).

Jenkins, John H., editor. *The Papers of the Texas Revolution, 1835-1836* (Austin: Presidial Press, 1973), Vol. II.

Jennett, Elizabeth LeNoir. *Biographical Directory of the Texan Conventions and Congresses* (Austin: No Publisher Given, 1941).

Jones, William M. *Texas Testimony Carved in Stone* (Houston: Scardino Printing, 1952).

Kendall, Dorothy Steinbomer. *Gentilz: Artist of the Old Southwest* (Austin: University of Texas Press, 1974).

Lester, Charles Edwards. *The Life of Sam Houston, The Hunter, Patriot and Statesman of Texas* (Philadelphia: J. E. Potter Co., circa 1867).

Linn, J. J. *Reminiscences of Fifty Years in Texas* (Austin: The Steck Co., 1935).

Lord, Clifford L., editor. *Keepers of the Past* (Chapel Hill: The University of North Carolina Press, 1965).

Lord, Walter. *A Time to Stand* (New York: Harper, 1961).

McComb, David G. *Houston: The Bayou City* (Austin: University of Texas Press, 1969).

Mason, Herbert Molloy, Jr. *Missions of Texas* (Birmingham, Ala.: Oxmoor House, 1974).

Miller, Thomas Lloyd. *Bounty and Donation Land Grants in Texas 1835-1838* (Austin: University of Texas Press, 1967).

Morrell, Z. N. *Flowers and Fruits in the Wilderness* (St. Louis: Commercial Printing Company, 1872).

Muir, Andrew Forest, editor. *Texas in 1837* (Austin: University of Texas Press, 1958).

Myers, John Myers. *The Alamo* (New York: E. P. Dutton & Company, 1948).

Newell, Chester. *History of the Revolution in Texas* (Austin: The Steck Company, 1935).

Perry, Carmen, translator and editor. *With Santa Anna in Texas* (College Station: Texas A&M Press, 1975).

Ramsdell, Charles. *San Antonio* (Austin: University of Texas Press, 1959).

Schroeder, Joseph J., Jr. *The Wonderful World of Ladies' Fashion* (Chicago: Follett Publishing Company, 1971).

Sibley, Marilyn McAdams. *The Port of Houston* (Austin: University of Texas Press, 1968).

Smithwick, Noah. *Evolution of a State* (Austin: Gammel Book Store, 1900).

Santos, Richard G. *Santa Anna's Campaign Against Texas, 1835-1836* (Waco: Texian Press, 1968).

Sowell, A. J. *Early Settlers and Indian Fighters of Southwest Texas* (New York: Argosy-Antiquarian Ltd., 1964).

_____. *Rangers and Pioneers of Texas* (New York: Argosy-Antiquarian Ltd., 1964).

Sutherland, John. *The Fall of the Alamo* (San Antonio: The Naylor Company, 1936).

Sweet, Alex. E. and J. Armoy Knox. *On a Mexican Mustang* (Hartford, Conn.: S. S. Scranton & Co., 1883).

Tinch, Helen Pearl. *Days of Colonial Texas* (Houston: Published Under Auspices of the American Museum Society of Houston Baptist College, 1967).

Tolbert, Frank X. *An Informal History of Texas* (New York: Harper & Brothers, 1951).

_____. *The Day of San Jacinto* (New York: McGraw-Hill Company, 1959).

Turner, Martha Anne. *The Life and Times of Jane Long* (Waco: Texian Press, 1969).

_____. *William Barret Travis, His Sword and His Pen* (Waco: Texian Press, 1972).

Van Orman, Richard A. *A Room for the Night* (Bloomington: Indiana University Press, 1966).

Watkins, Sue, editor. *One League to Each Wind* (Austin: Von Boeckmann-Jones, 1965).

Watson, Margaret. *Silver Theatre: Amusements of the Mining Frontier in Early Nevada, 1850-1864* (Glendale: The Arthur H. Clark Company, 1964).

Webb, Walter Prescott. *The Texas Rangers* (New York: Houghton Mifflin Company, 1935).

_____., editor. *The Handbook of Texas* (Austin: The Texas State Historical Association, 1952).

Weyand, Leonie Rummel and Houston Wade. *An Early History of Fayette County* (LaGrange: The LaGrange Journal Plant, 1936).

Wilcox, R. Turner. *The Mode in Costume* (New York: Charles Scribner's Sons, 1944).

Williamson, Roxanne Kuter. *Austin, Texas, An American Architectural History* (San Antonio: Trinity University Press, 1973).

Williams, Amelia and Eugene C. Barker, editors. *Writings of Sam Houston, 1836* (Austin: University of Texas Press, 1938-1943), Vol. 5.

Wisehart, M. K. *Sam Houston, American Giant* (Washington: Robert B. Luce, Inc., 1962).

Zuber, William Physick. *My Eighty Years in Texas* (Austin: University of Texas Press, 1971).

The Oxford English Dictionary (Oxford: Clarendon Press, 1961), Vol. I.

The World Book Encyclopedia (Chicago: Field Enterprises, Inc., 1948), Vol. 10.

THESES

Davie, Flora Agatha. *The Early History of Houston, Texas, 1836-1845,* Unpublished thesis, The University of Texas, August, 1940.

O'Banion, Maurine M. *The History of Caldwell County*, Unpublished thesis, The University of Texas, August, 1931.

ARTICLES

"Mrs. Dickenson Mother of the Babe of the Alamo," *Pioneer News-Observer,* November, 1970.

Barnes, Charles Merritt. "Alamo's Only Survivor," from the San Antonio *Express*, May 12, 19, 1907, reprinted in *Texana*, Vol. XI, No. 2, 1973.

Bennet, Miles S. "The Battle of Gonzales," *The Quarterly of the Texas State Historical Association,* Vol. II, No. 4, April, 1899.

Bishop, Curt. "Alamo Heroine Found Happiness in Austin." Austin *Times Herald,* Sept. 7, 1956.

_____. "Susannah Dickinson, The Alamo's Forgotten Heroine," *Texas Parade,* Vol. XXIV, No. 8, January, 1964.

Black, Roy S., Sr. "The Genesis of County Organization in the Western District of North Carolina and in The State of Tennessee." *The West Tennessee Historical Society Papers,* Vol. II, 1948.

DeShields, James T. "Colonial Times of Texas: Early Trials of DeWitt's Colonists," *Texas Magazine,* Vol. 1, No. 3, July, 1896.

Garwood, Ellen. "Early Texas Inns: A Study in Social Relationships," *The Southwestern Historical Quarterly,* Vol. LX, No. 2, October, 1956.

Halpenny, Marie. "Lady of the Alamo," *Texas Parade,* January, 1956.

Harris, Mrs. Dilue. "Reminiscence of Mrs. Dilue Harris," *The Southwestern Historical Association,* Vol. IV, pp. 179-182, July, 1900 to April, 1901.

Hart, Weldon. "Mother of Alamo Monument Is Due After 65 Years," Austin *American*, April 2, 1948.

Henderson,, Mary Virginia. "Minor Empresario Contracts for the Colonization of Texas, 1825-1834," *The Southwestern Historical Quarterly,* Vol. XXXI, No. 4, April, 1928.

Hogan, William Ransom. "Pamelia Mann: Texas Frontierswoman," *Southwest Review,* Vol. XX, No. 7, July, 1935.

Jung, Margetta. "Alamo's Heroine Gave Texas the Battle Cry Heard Over the World." Austin *American,* April 19, 1950.

Keasler, Jack. "Tenoxtitlan Yule Is Texas' Delight," Austin *American-Statesman*, Dec. 17, 1972.

Kelley, Dayton. "Susanna Dickinson," *Women of Texas* (Waco: Texian Press, 1972).

Kilman, Ed. "Texas Heartbeat," Houston *Post*, Sept. 10, 1961. Also January, 1959, from an undated clipping in the Barker History Center, The University of Texas, biographical file on Almeron and Susanna Dickinson.

Martindale, J. Henry. "Lady of the Alamo," *Texas Observer,* March 11, 1956.

_____. "Memory of a Cook," Austin *American,* Jan. 20, 1961.

_____. "These Are Only a Few of Our Early Pioneers," Lockhart *Post-Register,* May 6, 1948.

Menn, Alfred E. "Susan Dickenson, Alamo Defender," *The Dallas Morning News,* March 20, 1954.

Muir, Andrew Forest. "In Defense of Mrs. Mann," *Mexican Border Ballads and Other Lore,* edited by Mody C. Boatright

(Austin: Publication of the Texas Folklore Society, Vol. XX, 1946.

Red, William S. "Extracts from the Diary of W. Y. Allen, 1838-1839," *The Southwestern Historical Quarterly,* Vol. XVII (1913-1914).

Williams, Amelia. "Texas Collection," *The Southwestern Historical Quarterly,* Vol. XLIX, No. 4, April, 1946.

_____. "A Critical Study of the Siege of the Alamo and of the Personnel of Its Defenders," *The Southwestern Historical Quarterly,* Vol. XXXVII, 1934.

UNPUBLISHED MATERIALS

Ginsburg, David, "The Survivors of the Alamo," 12th Grade Unpublished Paper, Stephen F. Austin High School, Austin, Texas. Copy in the Austin Public Library.

Burkett, Nathan Boone. "Early Days in Texas," unfinished manuscript dictated at Moulton, Lavaca County, in April, 1895, to his son-in-law, John Hogwood. The manuscript is in The University of Texas Archives, Austin.

Notes, Charles Ramsdell to Mrs. R. E. Nitschke. In possession of Mrs. Nitschke, Austin.

Letter, E. A. Masur of Lockhart to Lockhart *Post-Register,* a copy of which is in the Louis W. Kemp Papers, General Biographical Notebook, DED-Di, The University of Texas Archives, Austin.

Letters, E. A. Masur of Lockhart to Boyce House, in Boyce House Papers, The University of Texas Archives, Sept. 26, 1945, to Nov. 6, 1946.

Interviews with Mrs. R. E. Nitschke, great granddaughter of Susanna Dickinson.

NEWSPAPERS

Bolivar (Tennessee) *Bulletin-Times,* June 5, 1975.

The Morning Star, 1839.

The Telegraph and Texas Register, 1836, 1838, 1843, 1845.

Austin *Daily Statesman,* 1876-1883, 1890.

San Antonio *Express,* 1881, 1883, 1884, 1890.

The Spirit of the Times, March 14, 1871.
Columbia *Telegraph,* Oct. 11, 1836.
Austin *American,* March 1, 1949.

DOCUMENTS

Bexar County Deeds, from clippings in the possession of Mrs. R. E. Nitschke, Austin.

Travis County Deeds, from clippings in the possession of Mrs. R. E. Nitschke, Austin.

Caldwell County Deed Books, Vols. F and G.

Bond and Marriage License of Susanna Wilkerson to Almeron Dickinson, Hardeman County, Tennessee, May 24, 1829. Copy in possession of Mrs. R. E. Nitschke.

Public Records, Hardeman County, Tennessee, Fitzhugh and Thomas J. Hardeman vs. John F. Robertson, April 10, 1829.

United States Census, Hardeman County, Tennessee, 1830.

United States Census, Harris County, Texas, 1850.

Susan Williams vs. John Williams, Republic of Texas, County of Harrisburg, District Court, March 10, 1838, Divorce Hearing.

House and Senate Journals of the Third Legislature, Texas, Regular Session, 1849-1850.

Journal of the House of Representatives, Republic of Texas, First Congress, First Session.

NOTES

[1]The 1830 United States Census for Hardeman County, Tennessee, shows several Wilkerson families in the county. The first head-of-household listed is that of Almeron Dickinson; the second is Benjamin Wilkerson, possibly the father of Susanna, in whose home was a male under five years of age and a female, possibly Benjamin's wife, between 20-30 years of age. On the Francis Wilkerson farm were a male under five, one between 10 and 15 years, one between 50-60, two females, one 5-15, and one 50-60. Too, five slaves made their home here. Another resident of the county was John B. Wilkerson, between 20-30 years of age. Nathaniel Wilkerson, between 50-60 years of age, headed a household consisting of one male under 5, one between 5-10 and one between 30-40. Richard Wilkerson, the owner of one slave, had a household consisting of a male under 5, two between 10-15, one between 40-50, three females between 5-10, one between 10-20, and one in the 50-60 age bracket.

A household operated by Mary Dickinson, 30-40 years of age, consisted of a male between 5-10 years, one between 10-15, and two females 5-10 years of age.

The census report for Hardeman County was filed November 24, 1830.

In the Middleburg vicinity of the county, in one of the oldest cemeteries, rest the remains of Lucinga Wilkinson, Sept. 2, 1806-July 7, 1828. The monument, a large one, was erected by her son David B. Wilkinson. An early historian of Hardeman County said that the woman was a member of the family of Susanna Wilkerson Dickinson. (Letter, Mr. and Mrs. Robert S. Owens, Bolivar, Tennessee, to Author, Jan. 21, 1975.)

[2]A letter from John R. Stracener, grand secretary, Grand Lodge, Free and Accepted Masons of Tennessee, Nashville, to the author, dated April 22, 1975, says, "We were unable to find a record of Almeron

Dickinson (Dickerson) in the old Clinton Lodge #54 at Bolivar." Stracener did indicate that "records prior to the Civil War are not all complete."

[3]Public records, Edward Fitzhugh and Thomas J. Hardeman vs. John F. Robertson, Friday, April 10, 1829.

[4]Bond, Hardeman County, Tennessee, signed by B. D. Johnston and Almeron Dickinson, May 24, 1829.

[5]Letter, Quinnie Armour, Bolivar, Tennessee, to Mrs. R. E. Nitschke, Austin, Texas, Jan. 18, 1868. An item in the Bolivar *Bulletin-Times*, June 5, 1975, discusses Spring Hill Cemetery, "about 5 miles south of Bolivar," "one of the oldest cemeteries in Hardeman County." One of the gravestones marks the burial place of Lucinga Wilkinson, who died in 1828.

[6]U.S. Census, Hardeman County, Tennessee, 1830.

CHAPTER TWO
Gonzales

[1]James Kerr was born in Kentucky and served two terms in the state senate of Missouri before moving to Texas in 1825. He was elected to the Congress of the Republic of Texas in 1838 and was author of a bill to prohibit dueling. (Sue Watkins, editor, *One League to Each Wind*, pp. 281, 341-343).

[2]Sue Watkins, ed. *One League to Each Wind;* (Austin: Von Boeckmann-Jones, 1965), p. 58. See also John Henry Brown, *Indian Wars and Pioneers of Texas* (Austin, 1895), p. 15.

[3](Ethel Zivley Rather, "DeWitt's Colony," *The Quarterly of the Texas State Historical Association*, VIII, No. 2 (October, 1904), p. 103).

[4]*Ibid.*, p. 105.

[5]A letter, James Kerr to Stephen F. Austin, Aug. 18, 1826, Austin Papers, Class D, No. 21, edited in Rather's article, "DeWitt's Colony," p. 105.

[6]Ethel Rather, "DeWitt's Colony," p. 106.

[7]*Ibid.*, p. 114.

[8]*Ibid.*, p. 136.

[9]*Ibid.*, pp. 140-141.

[10]Born in Kentucky, Mathew Caldwell came to Texas from Missouri. He represented Gonzales in the convention of 1836 and was one of the signers of the Declaration of Independence. President Mirabeau B. Lamar named him captain of a company of Rangers to defend Goliad. He participated in the Council House Fight, the Plum Creek Fight, and the Texan Santa Fe Expedition. He commanded a force which defeated Adrian Woll in the battle of Salado. *The Handbook of Texas*, I, p. 268.

[11]Andrew Forest Muir, editor, *Texas in 1837* (Austin: University of Texas Press, 1958), p. 89.

[12]Helen Pearl Tinch, *Days of Colonial Texas* (Houston: Under the Auspices of the American Museum Society of Houston Baptist College, 1967), p. 6.

[13]Tinch, *Days of Colonial Texas*, p. 12.

[14]Quoted in Helen Pearl Tinch, *Days of Colonial Texas*, but taken from Mrs. Pennybacker's *History of Texas*, and the original source is not identified.

[15]Notes from Charles Ramsdell.

[16]Nathan Boone Burkett, "Early Days in Texas," an unfinished manuscript dictated at Moulton, Lavaca County, April, 1895, to his son-in-law, John T. Hogwood. A typescript is in The University of Texas Archives, Barker History Center, Austin, Texas.

[17]Rather, p. 117. See also Mary Virginia Henderson, "Minor Empresario Contracts for the Colonization of Texas, 1825-1834," *The Southwestern Historical Quarterly*, Vol. XXXI, No. 4 (April, 1928), p. 301.

[18]Rather, p. 116.

[19]Rather, p. 117. See also Mary Virginia Henderson, "Minor Empresario Contracts for the Colonization of Texas, 1825-1834," p. 297.

[20]*Ibid.*, pp. 119-120.

[21]*Ibid.*, fn, p. 121, citing D. S. H. Darst, a resident of Gonzales from 1831.

[22]Patrick succeeded Fielding Porter as commissioner of Green C. DeWitt's colony in 1830 and continued in office until 1831. He was elected alcalde in 1832. *The Handbook of Texas*, Vol. II, p. 345.

[23]Charts in Ethel Rather, pp. 168-170.

[24]Rather, p. 122.

[25]*Ibid.*, pp. 120-121.

[26]*Ibid.*, pp. 122-123.

[27]A. J. Sowell, *Early Settlers and Indian Fighters*, p. 410.

[28]Noah Smithwick, *From Evolution of a State*, pp. 15-16, as cited by John Q. Anderson, *Tales of Frontier Texas*, 1830-1860 (Dallas: Southern Methodist University Press, 1966), pp. 87-89.

[29]Creed Taylor, born in Tennessee, was in Bastrop, Texas, when he joined a company under Robert M. Coleman and John James Tumlinson to fight in the battle of Concepcion and in the siege at Bexar. In January, 1836, he was a scout at San Patricio, and on March 1, joined the Texas forces at Gonzales and accompanied his mother on the 'Runaway Scrape.' He was a member of the Texas Rangers under John Coffee (Jack) Hays. He took part in the Indian fight at Bandera Pass and in the battle of Salado. Under Hays, he fought in the battles at Palo Alto, Resaca de la Palma, Monterrey, and Bueno Vista in the War with Mexico. (*The Handbook of Texas*, Vol. II, p. 715) See Also A. J. Sowell, *Early Settlers and Indian Fighters*, Vol. II, pp. 805-810.

[30]Sowell, *Early Settlers and Indian Fighters*, p. 808.

[31]Sowell, *Rangers and Pioneers of Texas* (New York: Argosy-Antiquarian Ltd., 1964, p. 111). See also A. J. Sowell, *Early Settlers and Indian Fighters*, p. 437.

[32]Sowell, *Rangers and Pioneers of Texas*, pp. 111-112.

[33]Sowell, *Rangers and Pioneers of Texas*, pp. 111-115. See the same story with additional facts in Sowell's *Early Settlers and Indian Fighters*, pp. 434-440.

[34]Sowell, *Rangers and Pioneers of Texas*, p. 118.

[35]*Ibid.*, p. 119. Another version of the same story appears in Sowell, *Early Settlers and Indian Fighters*, pp. 410-411.

[36]Sowell, *Rangers and Pioneers of Texas*, pp. 123-124.

[37]Miller's home was the meeting place of the *ayuntamiento* during 1834.

[38]Rather, Appendix VI, minutes of the *ayuntamiento*, p. 185.

[39]Rather, pp. 181-188.

[40]*Ibid*., p. 128.

[41]*Ibid*., p. 137.

[42]A plaque on the interior of the Gonzales Museum and Amphitheatre honors the old Eighteen:

> These 18 men constituted the Texian's only line of defense in this hour of destiny. By advising with Alcalde Andrew Ponton the 18 delayed for two days 150 Mexican dragoons sent by their government to demand the Gonzales cannon.

> It was the strategy of these men that allowed time for colonists to mass volunteers that drove back the enemy in "The Battle of Gonzales." At this battle was given to the world a new battle flag and a new war cry, "Come and Take It," and was started the successful Texan Revolution against the Mexican Government.

THE OLD EIGHTEEN

Captain Albert Martin, Jacob C. Darst, Winslow Turner, Wm. W. Arrington, Gravis Fulcher, George Davis, John Sowell, Benjamin Fuqua, Thomas Jackson, James B. Hinds, Thomas R. Miller, Valentine Bennet, Ezekiel Williams, Simeon Bateman, Joseph D. Clements, Almaron Dickerson, Charles Mason, Almond Cottle. William M. Jones, *Texas Testimony Carved in Stone* (Houston: Scardino Printing, 1952), p. 190.

[43]George Washington Davis was born in Tennessee March 20, 1806. He came to Texas in 1831. History records him as a participant in the Convention of 1833 and in the Consultation, in the Battle for Gonzales, in the siege of Bexar, in the Battle of Concepcion, and in the Battle of San Jacinto. *The Handbook of Texas*, Vol. I, p. 470.

[44]Miles S. Bennet visited the scene of the battle with his father, Mayor Valentine Bennet, on July 4, 1838. He writes of this visit in "The Battle of Gonzales," *The Quarterly of the Texas Historical Association*, Vol. II, No. 4 (April, 1899), p. 313.

[45]Miles S. Bennet, p. 314.

[46]*Ibid*., p. 315.

[47]James T. DeShields, *Tall Men with Long Rifles*, p. 17.

[48]*Ibid.*, p. 18.

[49]*Ibid.*, p. 17.

[50]Notice the discrepancy. Some authorities have called it a brass cannon.

[51]Noah Smithwick, *The Evolution of a State*, (Austin: Gammel Book Store, 1900), p. 102.

[52]James T. DeShields, *Tall Men with Long Rifles*, pp. 26-27.

[53]Miles S. Bennet, p. 315.

[54]*The Handbook of Texas*, I, p. 470.

[55]Joseph Washington Elliott Wallace, Pennsylvania born, came to Texas in 1830 and settled at Gonzales. *The Handbook of Texas*, II, p. 856.

[56]James T. DeShields, *Tall Men with Long Rifles*, p. 19.

[57]Donna Lee Dickerson, *A Typestick of Texas History* (Austin: Department of Journalism Development Fund, The University of Texas at Austin, 1972), p. 20.

[58]*Ibid.*, p. 21.

[59]Noah Smithwick, *The Evolution of a State*, pp. 102-104.

[60]*Ibid.*, p. 107.

[61]Miles S. Bennet, p. 315.

[62]Smithwick, *The Evolution of a State*, pp. 109-110.

[63]James T. DeShields, *Tall Men with Long Rifles*, pp. 31-32.

[64]*Ibid.*, pp. 32-33.

[65]Smithwick, *The Evolution of a State*, p. 111.

[66]M. K. Wisehart, *Sam Houston American Giant*, p. 131.

[67]Item 1086, L. Smither to Stephen F. Austin, Gonzales, Nov. 4, 1835, in John H. Jenkins, editor, *The Papers of the Texas Revolution*, Vol. II, p. 318.

[68]Item 1087, L. Smither to Stephen F. Austin, Gonzales, Nov. 4, 1835, in John H. Jenkins, editor, *The Papers of the Texas Revolution*, 1835-1836 (Austin: Presidial Press, 1973), Vol. 2, p. 319.

[69]Smithwick, *The Evolution of a State*, p. 113.

[70]*Ibid.*, p. 115.

[71]M. K. Wisehart, *Sam Houston American Giant*, p. 134.

CHAPTER THREE
San Antonio Years

[1]Ramón Musquiz was known throughout Texas as a Mason. On Feb. 21, 1828, he had acknowledged receipt of a petition from Masons in San Felipe de Austin seeking to establish a chapter in that community. Musquiz answered that he was "particularly pleased to be informed how many brethren you found in that district" and sent the petition on to higher authorities. James D. Carter, *Masonry in Texas* (Waco: The Committee on Masonic Education and Service for the Grand Lodge of Texas, A. F. and A. M., 1955), p. 235.

[2]Walter Prescott Webb, ed., *The Handbook of Texas*, II, P. 253.

[3]Charles Ramsdell, *San Antonio* (Austin: University of Texas Press, 1959), p. 68. See also Richard G. Santos, *Santa Anna's Campaign Against Texas, 1835-1836* (Waco: Texian Press, 1973), p. 81.

[4]Dr. John Sutherland, a Virginian practicing medicine in Alabama, decided in 1835 to settle in Texas. He arrived at San Felipe in December, took the oath of allegiance to the Provisional government, and joined the company of soldiers under Capt. William Patten. He and ten other volunteers made their way to San Antonio.

[5]James T. DeShields, *Tall Men with Long Rifles* (San Antonio: The Naylor Company, 1971), pp. 150-151.

[6]*Ibid.*, p. 151.

[7]Where Navarro Street bridge is now located.

[8]Thomas William Ward, born in Ireland in 1807, was a volunteer with Ben Milam. On the day that Milam was killed, Ward lost a leg, severed by a cannon ball, and legend has it that Ward's limb and Milam's body were interred in the same grave. Ward, although crippled, went to New Orleans to recruit for the Texian cause. He returned to Texas with a company of volunteers. After the Battle of San Jacinto, he became an architect and contractor in Houston, accepting an assignment

137

to build the temporary capitol. He later became mayor of Austin and served in a number of state positions. *The Handbook of Texas*, II, p. 861.

⁹Charles Ramsdell, *San Antonio*, p. 6.

¹⁰Massachusetts born, Nathaniel C. Lewis came to Texas in 1830, becoming a merchant at Indianola and then in San Antonio. In 1836, he is believed to have slipped into the Alamo with supplies for the defenders and has been called the last Anglo-American to leave the fortress before the massacre. He later served the Texas Army as a scout and in 1839-40 was a member of the House of Representatives of the Fourth Congress. He carried on a large freight business between El Paso and San Antonio. *The Handbook of Texas*, II, p. 53.

¹¹Charles Ramsdell, *San Antonio*, p. 69.

¹²*Ibid*.

¹³James Wakefield Burke, *Missions of Old Texas* (Cranbury, N. J.: A. S. Barnes and Co., 1971), p. 142.

¹⁴James Wakefield Burke, *Missions of Old Texas* , pp. 143-144.

¹⁵*The Handbook of Texas*, Vol. I, p. 22.

¹⁶Martha Anne Turner, *William Barret Travis*, p. 232.

¹⁷*Ibid*., p. 26.

¹⁸*Ibid*., p. 59.

¹⁹Robert E. Davis, *Diary of William B. Travis* (Waco: Texian Press, 1966), p. xii.

²⁰Rebecca Cummings was the daughter of Mrs. Rebecca Cummings, one of the Old Three Hundred Colonists of Stephen F. Austin's Colony. Upon the death of her mother, the younger Rebecca managed the family plantation near San Felipe. *The Handbook of Texas*, I, p. 445.

²¹Martha Anne Turner, *The Life and Times of Jane Long* (Waco: Texian Press, 1969), p. iii.

²²Now on display in the Alamo, the ring has brought some discussion. T. H. McGregor of Austin wrote Ed Kilman, Houston columnist, the following explanation:
Prior to the Civil War she (Angelina Dickinson) lived in Galveston and was friendly with Jim Britton who at that time was connected with the operation of a train. She gave the ring to

Britton. Britton had been raised at Lebanon, Tennessee, and had been an associate and close friend of Paul F. Anderson, a brother of my Mother and the late Mrs. S. S. Ashe of Houston. On the breaking out of the War Anderson and Britton returned to Lebanon where Anderson became a Captain and Britton a Lieutenant of the "Cedar Shakes," a company in Baxter Smith's Fourth Tennessee Regiment which was brigaded with the Texas Rangers. Anderson afterwards became a Colonel and Britton a Captain in the Confederate Army. Anderson had a younger brother who was a Junior Lieutenant under Britton DeWitt Anderson. Britton gave the Travis ring to DeWitt Anderson who wore it until his death in 1902 at Marianna, Arkansas, at which time the ring came into my possession. (Letter, T. H. McGregor to Ed Kilman, Jan. 21, 1942, in L. W. Kemp Papers, The University of Texas Archives.) T. H. McGregor gave the ring to his son Douglas McGregor, Houston attorney, who presented it to the Alamo museum. (Letter, E. A. B., Houston, Oct. 11, 1961, in Barker Library, The University of Texas, Dickinson file).

[23] Amos Pollard, born in Massachusetts in 1803, received medical training in New York. He came to Texas in 1835 and settled at Gonzales. *The Handbook of Texas*, vol. II, p. 390.

[24] Martha Anne Turner, *The Life and Times of Jane Long*, p. 197.

[25] *Ibid.*, p. 251.

[26] John Myers, *The Alamo* (New York: E. P. Dutton and Co., 1948), pp. 92, 93, 95, 103, 106.

[27] Joe, Travis's servant, as reported in Edward G. Rohrbough, "How Jim Bowie Died," *In the Shadow of History* (Austin: Texas Folklore Society, 1939), p. 53.

[28] A. J. Sowell, *Rangers and Pioneers of Texas*, p. 141.

[29] Dr. John Sutherland, *The Fall of the Alamo* (San Antonio: The Naylor Company, 1936), p. 40.

[30] *Ibid.*, p. 40, fn 40.

[31] A. J. Sowell, *Rangers and Pioneers of Texas*, pp. 138-139.

[32] *Ibid.*, pp. 140-141.

[33] As Enrique Esparza recounted the story:

"We were all marched off to the house of Señor Musquiz. Here all of the women were placed under guard. Musquiz owned a *suerte* on South Alamo Street not very far from where the Beethoven Hall now is. My mother and father were well acquainted with the Musquiz family. At about 8 o'clock we became very hungry, up to then not having been given any food. My mother, being familiar with the premises, began to look about for food for herself and her children as well as her other comrades. While she was doing so, Musquiz told her that it was dangerous for her to be moving about and leaving the place and room in which she was under guard. She told him she did not care whether she was under guard or not, she was going to have something to eat for herself, her children and her companions whom she intended to feed if Santa Anna did not feed his prisoners. Musquiz admonished her to silence and told her to be patient and he would get them some food from his own store.

"After urging my mother not to leave the room, Musquiz disappeared and went to his pantry, where he got quite a quantity of provisions and brought them to the room in which the prisoners, some ten or a dozen in number were and distributed the food among them. There was some coffee as well as bread and meat. I recollect that I ate heartily, but my mother ate sparingly.

"We were kept at Musquiz's house until 3 o'clock in the afternoon when the prisoners were taken to Military Plaza.'' (Charles Merritt Barnes, "Alamo's Only Survivor," from San Antonio *Express*, May 12, 19, 1907, *Texana*, Vol. XI, No. 2, 1973.

[34]James D. Carter, *Masonry in Texas* (Waco: Grand Lodge, 1955), p. 276-277.

[35]Dr. Joseph E. Field, *Three Years in Texas* (Greenfield, Mass: 1836), as cited in John Jenkins, editor, *Papers of the Texas Revolution*, vol. 5, pp. 4,362.

With Santa Anna in Texas, A Personal Narrative of the Revolution by Jose Enrique de la Peña, translated and edited by Carmen Perry (College Station: Texas A&M Press, 1975), pp. 53-54, has a different version of the final hours of Davy Crockett. De la Peña says that Crockett came through the Alamo conflict alive and was ordered executed by Santa Anna. Some of the men around the Mexican leader ''. . . with swords in hand, fell upon these unfortunate, defenseless men just as a tiger leaps upon his prey. Though tortured before they were killed, these unfortunates died without complaining and without humiliating themselves before their torturers.''

[36]Enrique Esparza supports the story, recalling that Mrs. Alsbury and her sister Mrs. Gertrudis Cantu were taken before Santa Anna. He wrote:

"They took my mother, her babe, my brothers and I to another part of the building where there were other women and children all huddled. Another of the women had a babe at her breast. This was Mrs. Dickinson. There was an old woman in there. They called her Donna Petra. This was the only name I ever knew her by. With her was a young girl, Trinidad Saucedo, who was very beautiful. Mrs. Alsberry [sic] and her sister were there also and several other women, young girls and little boys."

"Mrs. Dickinson, the wife of Lieutenant Dickinson, the woman whom I told you, like my mother, had a babe at her breast, was the next to be summoned before Santa Anna. He spent some time in questioning her after which he dismissed her.

"My mother was next called before the dictator. When she appeared before him my baby sister pressed closely to her bosom. I with my brother followed her into his presence. My brother was clinging to her skirt, but I stood to one side and behind her. I watched every move and listened to every word spoken. Santa Anna asked her name. She gave it . . . . (He gave her a blanket and two silver dollars as he dismissed her. Also to the other women brought before him.) "Alamo's Only Survivor," by Charles Merritt Barnes, from the San Antonio *Express*, May 12, 19, 1907, *Texana*, Vol. XI, No. 2, 1973.

[37]Cleburne Smith, *Deaf Smith Incredible Texas Spy* (Waco: Texian Press, 1973), pp. 52-53.

[38]James D. Carter, *Masonry in Texas* (Waco: Published by the Committee on Masonic Education and Service for the Grand Lodge of Texas A.F. and A.M., 1955), pp. 276-277.

[39]Columbia *Telegraph*, Oct. 11, 1836.

[40]The source obviously was in error. The daughter escaped with Susanna Dickinson.

[41]Sam Houston to J. W. Fannin, from Gonzales, March 11, 1836, cited in Amelia Williams and Eugene C. Barker, editors, *Writings of Sam Houston, 1836* (Austin: University of Texas Press, 1938-43), Vol. 5, pp. 364-365.

[42]M. K. Wisehart, *Sam Houston American Giant*, pp. 175-177.

[43]Sarah Nash of Nash Creek married John Bruno and moved to Houston, where they settled on a spread of land. Later they sold their

Houston holdings for $118, moved to Gonzales, and invested the money in 1,280 acres. Interview with Jeff Allen, a grandson of the John Brunos, by Mrs. R. E. Nitschke, Jr., June 22, 1941.

[44]*Ibid*.

[45]William F. Gray, *From Virginia to Texas, 1835: Diary of Col. William F. Gray* (Houston: Fletcher Young Co., 1965), p. 137.

[46]*Telegraph and Texas Register*, March 24, 1836.

[47]Charles Newell, *History of the Revolution*, p. 88.

[48]Austin *American*, April 19, 1950.

[49]*Ibid*.

[50]Zuber, William P., *My Eighty Years in Texas*, edited by Janis Boyle Mayfield, (Austin, University of Texas Press, 1971), p. 53.

[51]J. J. Linn, *Reminiscences of Fifty Years in Texas* (Austin: The Steck Co., 1935), p. 144.

[52]Susanna Dickinson interview with Charles W. Evers, March 14, 1878, printed in *Frontier Times*, April, 1929.

[53]Cleburne Huston, *Deaf Smith, Incredible Texas Spy*, p. 52.

[54]*Ibid*., p. 53.

[55]*Ibid*., p. 1.

[56]Walter Lord, *A Time to Stand* (New York: Harper & Brothers, 1961), p. 126.

[57]James T. DeShields, *Tall Men with Long Rifles*, pp. 129-130.

[58]Leonie Rummel Weyand and Houston Wade, *An Early History of Fayette County*, (La Grange: no publisher, 1936), p. 126.

[59]Cleburne Huston, *Deaf Smith, Incredible Texas Spy*, p. 53.

[60]Leonie Runnel Weyand and Houston Wade, *An Early History of Fayette County* (LaGrange: No publisher named, 1936), p. 126.

[61]Charles Edwards Lester, *The Life of Sam Houston, The Hunter Patriot and Statesman of Texas* (Philadelphia: E. Potter Co., circa 1867), pp. 95-96.

[62]*Ibid*.

[63]Wisehart, *Sam Houston American Giant*, p. 181.

[64]*Papers of the Texas Revolution*, Vol. 5, p. 82.

[65]Possibly Private Hadden William Parker, who escaped from the Alamo but was found by Major Benjamin J. White and taken into the settlements along the Brazos, pp. 121-122, *Papers of the Texas Revolution*, Vol. 6.

[66]*Ibid*.

CHAPTER FOUR
Houston

[1]Mrs. Dilue Harris, ''The Reminiscences of Mrs. Dilue Harris,'' *The Quarterly of the Texas Historical Association*, IV, pp. 179-182.

[2]Francis R. Lubbock, *Six Decades in Texas*, edited by C. W. Raines, (Austin: Ben C. Jones and Company, 1900), p. 45.

[3]*The Journals of the House of Representatives of the Republic of Texas*, First Congress, First Session, lists Houston, Matagorda, Washington, Velasco, Quintana, Nacogdoches, Hidalgo, Refugio, Fort Bend, Goliad, Groce's Retreat, Bexar, Columbia, San Patricio, Brazoria, and Orozimbo.

[4]American Guide Series, *Houston: A Complete Guide and History* (Houston: The Anson Jones Press, 1942), pp. 37-40, citing Francis White Johnson's *A History of Texas and Texans*.

[5]Francis R. Lubbock, *Six Decades in Texas*, p. 46.

[6]A. Pat Daniels, *Texas Avenue at Main Street* (Houston: Allen Press, 1964), p. 4.

[7]Jeff Allen, interviewed by Mrs. R. E. Nitschke on June 22, 1941, recalled conversations with his grandmother, Sarah Nash Bruno, in whose home Susanna stopped after leaving the Alamo. The Brunos and Susanna and her baby made their way to Nash Creek. After the Battle of San Jacinto, the Bruno family returned to Gonzales. Allen did not know whether Mrs. Dickinson was with his family but believes she was not.

[8]Max Freund, editor, *Gustav Dresel's Journal* (Austin: University of Texas Press, 1954), p. 32.

[9]*Telegraph and Texas Register*, Nov. 2, 1836.

[10]George W. Wright, a native of Tennessee, came to Texas with his father's family in their keelboat. He and an older brother went to school in Kentucky but returned to live in Texas. Wright was elected a first

lieutenant in Captain John Hart's company of mounted men, but before his black Spanish mule could deliver him to Houston's forces, the battle of San Jacinto was over. He was chosen to represent Red River County in the House of the First Congress. Elizabeth LeNoir Jennett, *Biographical Directory of the Texan Conventions and Congresses*, (Austin: No publisher indicated, 1941), p. 195.

[11]Green, native of North Carolina, was educated at West Point. He was elected to his state's General Assembly, served in the State Legislature in Florida, and was present at the first session of the First Congress of the Republic of Texas. The following year he was elected to the Senate. Later he was in the Senate of California. He became a Major General of the California militia. (Elizabeth LeNoir Jennett, *Conventions and Congresses*, p. 91).

[12]A statesman and soldier born in Tennessee, Bunton represented Bastrop County in the First Congress. He had fought in the Battle of San Jacinto, signed the Declaration of Independence, and was a delegate to the Constitutional Convention in 1836. (Elizabeth LeNoir Jennett, *Conventions and Congresses*, p. 58).

[13]Robison came to Texas from Florida. Four months after attending the first session of the first Congress, he and his brother were delivering a wagonload of supplies when they were killed by Indians. (Elizabeth LeNoir Jennett, *Conventions and Congresses*, p. 161).

[14]Virginia born, Archer had served in that state's legislature before relocating in Texas. In Texas, he was Brazoria's delegate to the First Congress. He was speaker during the second session. (Elizabeth LeNoir Jennett, *Conventions and Congresses*, p. 44).

[15]Mosely Baker, born in Virginia and educated in Alabama, became a journalist before moving to Texas. (Elizabeth LeNoir Jennett, *Conventions and Congresses*, pp. 48-49).

[16]Transcribed from the original document by Edwin A. Bonewitz, Houston, August 18, 1958, a copy of which is in the Biographical File at Barker History Center, The University of Texas, Austin. The original is addressed to the Honorable District Judge, County of Harrisburg, Republic of Texas, March 10, 1838.

[17]*The Handbook of Texas*, Vol. II, p. 913.

[18]Gifford White, editor, *The 1840 Census of the Republic of Texas* (Austin: Pemberton Press, 1966), p. 24.

[19]*Ibid.*, p. 41.

[20]An 1814 definition of *abortion* is "arrestment of development of any organ so that it either remains a mere rudiment or is entirely shrivelled up or absorbed." *The Oxford English Dictionary*, (Oxford: Clarendon Press, 1961), p. 28.

[21]Edward H. Winfield, a native of Virginia, came to Texas in 1835 and served with the Texas Army as regimental quartermaster and major. He was released from service June 23, 1836. By 1838 he was secretary of the Houston board of health. He also served as tax assessor of Harris County, clerk of the district court of the Second Judicial District, and assistant secretary of the Senate for the adjourned session of the Second Congress. He lived in Mexico several months, served under Captain J. B. Robertson on the Somervell Expedition of 1842, and represented his district in the Third Legislature, 1849-1850. *The Handbook of Texas*, Vol. II, p. 923.

[22]Flora Agatha Davie, *The Early History of Houston, Texas*, 1836-1845. Unpublished thesis at The University of Texas, August, 1940, p. 44.

[23]A. Pat Daniels, *Texas Avenue at Main Street*, p. 4.

[24]W. B. Redd to Mirabeau B. Lamar, May 23, 1837, in *The Papers of Mirabeau Buonaparte Lamar*, edited by C. A. Gulick, Jr., and others. (Austin: Von Boeckmann-Jones, 1921), Vol. I, pp. 552-54.

[25]O. F. Allen, *The City of Houston from Wilderness to Wonder*, (Temple: Privately printed, 1936), p. 6.

[26]*Ibid.*, p. 7.

[27]A. Pat Daniels, p. 5.

[28]Z. N. Morrell, *Flowers and Fruits in the Wilderness* (St. Louis: Commercial Printing Company), p. 66.

[29]Kelsey H. Douglass to wife, Dec. 10, 1837, in The University of Texas Archives, Austin. Kelsey N. Douglass Papers, 1837-1840.

[30]Andrew Forest Muir, "In Defense of Mrs. Mann," *Mexican Border Ballads and Other Lore*, edited by Mody C. Boatright (Austin: Publication of the Texas Folklore Society, XXI, 1945), pp. 117-118. See also William Ransom Hogan, "Pamelia Mann: Texas Frontierswoman," *Southwest Review* XX (September, 1935), pp. 360-370; Richard A. Van Orman, *A Room for the Night*, (Bloomington: Indiana University Press, 1966), and Ellen Garwood, "Early Texas Inns: A Study in Social Relationships," *Southwest Historical Quarterly*, LX: 2 (October, 1956).

[31]When her oxen had been requisitioned by Sam Houston during his retreat before the Mexican armies, Mrs. Mann angrily unhitched the beasts and drove them back to her farm. She was charged a number of times with counterfeiting, immorality, larceny, and assault to murder, and on one occasion she was convicted of forgery. (American Guide Series, *Houston: A Complete Guide and History*, p. 222).

[32]*Morning Star*, September 25, 1939.

[33]Max Freund, editor, *Gustav Dresel's Journal*, p. 78.

[34]Crawford Street was named in honor of Joseph Tucker Crawford who visited Texas in 1837 in order to report to the British government on conditions in the Republic.

[35]Ed Kilman, "Texas Heartbeat," Houston *Post*, Jan., 1959, Undated clipping in the Biographical file of Barker History Center, The University of Texas, Austin.

[36]An 1837 and 1838 account book kept by Doswell and Adams Store as cited in Flora Agatha Davie, *The Early History of Houston, Texas, 1836-1845,* unpublished thesis at The University of Texas, August, 1940.

[37]*The Morning Star*, Sept. 11, 1839.

[38]*Telegraph and Texas Register*, Oct. 28, 1837.

[39]Francis R. Lubbock, *Six Decades in Texas*, p. 67.

[40]*Telegraph and Texas Register*, Feb. 24, 1838.

[41]William S. Red, Extracts from the Diary of W. Y. Allen, *The Southwestern Historical Quarterly*, XVIII, p. 294.

[42]*The Handbook of Texas*, I, p. 132.

[43]*Telegraph and Texas Register*, August 11, 1838.

[44]Edward Stiff, *The Texan Emigrant* (Waco: Texian Press, 1968), pp. 82-83.

[45]Flora Agatha Davie, *The Early History of Houston, Texas, 1835-1845*, unpublished thesis at The University of Texas, Austin, August, 1940, p. 175.

[46]*Ibid.*

[47]*Telegraph and Texas Register*, Dec. 15, 1838.

146

[48]Marriage Volume A, page 77, Harrisburg County, Texas.

[49]Ed Kilman, Houston *Post*, Jan. 1859, undated clipping in Barker History Collection, The University of Texas.

[50]*Houston*, p. 52.

[51]Ferdinand Roemer, *Roemer's Texas* (San Antonio: Standard Printing Company, 1935), p. 64.

[52]Roemer, p. 67.

[53]The name is spelled variously Bellows, Bellis, Belles.

[54]U. S. Census, 1850, p. 37.

[55]The Rev. Charles Gillett was born in Connecticut about 1820. He became rector of the Christ Church in Houston in 1843, conducting his first services in a building owned by the Presbyterians. In the summer of 1844, he made a trip to the United States to raise funds for a church building for his own denomination. He made frequent missionary trips through central Texas and was secretary of the convention which formed the first Protestant Episcopal diocese in Texas. *The Handbook of Texas*, Vol. I, p. 691.

[56]*Telegraph and Texas Register*, May 14, 1845.

[57]U. S. Census, Texas, Harris County, 1850, p. 37, dwelling 353.

[58]Francis Moore, Jr., Massachusetts born, studied medicine, practiced law, taught school, and edited a newspaper. From 1839 to 1842, he represented Harris, Liberty and Galveston Counties in the Senate of the Fourth, Fifth, and Sixth Congresses of Texas. He was state geologist, 1859-1860. *The Handbook of Texas*, Vol. II, p. 229.

[59]James W. Scott was born in Richmond, Va., and arrived in Texas in 1836 and he was confirmed as paymaster in the Texas Army. In 1840, he was in the auction and commission business in Houston. He represented Harris County in the Third and Fourth Legislatures, 1849-1853. *The Handbook of Texas*, II, p. 582.

[60]Georgia J. Burleson, *The Life and Writings of Rufus C. Burleson*, (Privately printed, 1901), pp. 739-740.

[61]Thomas Lloyd Miller, *Bounty and Donation Land Grants of Texas, 1835-1888* (Austin: University of Texas Press, 1967), pp. 226, 758. The Patent was 6 Vol. 8 Abst 117, GLO File Fan Bty 305.

[62]Walter Prescott Webb, editor, *The Handbook of Texas*, (Austin: Texas State Historical Association, 1952), I, p. 21.

[63]Walter Lord, in *A Time to Stand*, says David's father was a wealthy Harrisburg, Pa., canal man "who claimed friendship with Sam Houston." The senior Cummings "bought a box of rifles from the state arsenal and sent them along with the boy, (p. 46) who delivered the crate." (p. 82).

[64]Grant no. 535 awarded David P. Cumming's heirs 640 acres registered Feb. 26, 1857, approved and delivered Oct. 26, 1857.

[65]Harris County Marriage Books, B, p. 299. No. 274-17-0302 copy.

[66]Burleson, *The Life and Writings of Dr. Rufus C. Burleson*, p. 740.

[67]DeShields, *Tall Men with Long Rifles*, pp. 189-190.

[68]Houston *Telegraph*, July 30, 1869.

[69]James Wilson Henderson, a native of Tennessee, arrived in Texas shortly after the Battle of San Jacinto. He became a land surveyor in Harris County, then studied law and was admitted to the Bar in 1842. He won a seat in the House of Representatives in 1843 and was reelected in 1844. He was chosen speaker of the House in 1847, defeating former President Mirabeau B. Lamar. Henderson was elected lieutenant governor in 1851, and when Bell resigned in 1853, Henderson became governor. *The Handbook of Texas*, I, p. 796.

[70]No. 3618, Peter Bellows vs. Susanna Bellows, 11th Judicial Court, Granted 6/5/57, recorded Vol. H, page 479, Minutes of Courts, Harris County.

[71]P. B. George, born in New Hampshire, was listed in the U. S. Census of 1850 as 39 years of age.

[72]G. Gerson was a surviving partner of Gerson and Ephraim firm (p. 480, Book H, Minutes of District Court, Harris Co., June 15, 1857).

[73]District Court Minutes, Book H, pp. 479-480, Case 3618.

[74]Filed May 1, 1857, in District Clerk's office.

[75]May 1, 1857 document.

[76]L. W. Kemp, General Biographical Notebook, *Ded* to *Di*, The University of Texas Archives, Austin.

CHAPTER FIVE
Lockhart

[1]Maurine M. O'Banion, *The History of Caldwell County*, Unpublished Master's thesis at The University of Texas, August, 1931, p. 104.

[2]Henry H. Field's Diary, as quoted in the Lockhart *Post-Register*, November, 1972.

[3]*Ibid*.

[4]J. Henry Martindale, "Lady of the Alamo," *Texas Observer*, March 14, 1956.

[5]E. A. Masur, Letter to L. W. Kemp, Aug. 24, 1938, in Kemp Files, The University of Texas Archives, Austin.

[6]Kemp Papers.

[7]*The Dallas Morning News*, March 9, 1930.

[8]J. Henry Martindale, "Memory of a Cook," Austin *American*, Jan. 20, 1961.

[9]Sam J. R. McDowell was born in Tennessee in 1824. (J. Henry Martindale, "These Are Only a Few of Our Early Pioneers," Lockhart *Post-Register*, May 6, 1948.

[10]Confusion continues concerning Rose. *The Handbook of Texas*, a standard reference work, has no information on a James Rose. The only Rose in the Alamo is identified as Moses Rose, a native of France, who came to Texas and worked as a day laborer in sawmills and as a teamster around Nacogdoches until October, 1835, when he went to San Antonio. It was Rose who elected to leave the Alamo March 3, 1836, when he learned that the Texian cause was hopeless. By eluding the Mexican forces, he was able to escape to Grimes County. He later settled in Nacogdoches, where he operated a butcher shop until 1842. Moses Rose was described as a swarthy man with black hair. *The Handbook of Texas*, Vol. II, p. 503. Walter Lord, in *A Time to Stand*, however, says James M. Rose, "the hot-tempered, sandy-haired nephew of Ex-President Madison," (p. 46) was a friend of Davy Crockett. (p. 54) Lord says that Rose "barely escaped the grasping hands of a Mexican officer" when he and several other Texians on Feb. 25 set fire to buildings outside the Alamo. (p. 109) Rose, "who stammered when excited," (p. 114) was called by the author "an impeccable hero." (p. 201).

[11]Caldwell County Records, Vol. F, p. 164.

[12]Caldwell County Records, Deed Book, Vol. F, p. 130.

[13]Austin *American*, Aug. 27, 1961.

[14]Henry Warnell, "a freckled, red-headed little jockey," who "drank hard, talked fast, and chewed mountains of tobacco," was in Arkansas before coming to Texas. (Walter Lord, *A Time to Stand*, p. 23. He, in the words of Walter Lord, "married (or didn't marry a girl in Lewis County . . . found himself a father . . . decided it was time to move on to Texas." (p. 24).

[15]Grant No. 400 awarded the heirs of Henry Warnell ⅔ league and one labor, HR 960 and bounty and 640 acres of Donation Grant, issued May 25, 1860.

[16]*House Journal*, p. 165.

[17]*Ibid*.

[18]*The Handbook of Texas*, Vol. I, p. 641. Franklin was the first man to hold a judicial position in the Republic of Texas. When the *Packet*, a brig owned by a U.S. Citizen, was captured by the *Invincible*, Texian officials were apprehensive of what the affair might do to American sympathy. To have the matter investigated, the government created a judicial district and appointed Franklin district judge. He represented Galveston County in the Legislature.

[19]*House Journal*, p. 262.

[20]*Ibid*., p. 276.

[21]Keenan represented Montgomery County in the First and Second Legislatures and was Speaker of the House, 1849 to 1850. *The Handbook of Texas*, Vol. I, pp. 940-941.

[22]Guy Morrison Bryan was boarding with Josiah H. Bell and attending school taught by Thomas J. Pilgrim in March, 1836, when he was selected courier for the letter William B. Travis wrote at the Alamo. He carried the message from Bell's Landing to Brazoria and Velasco. *The Handbook of Texas*, Vol. I, p. 233.

[23]Reference is to Santa Anna, more frequently called The Napoleon of the West.

[24]Known as "The Babe of the Alamo Speech," the address was delivered by Bryan sometime between Dec. 14-18, 1849.

[25]*The Handbook of Texas*, Vol. I, pp. 940-941.

[26]James Charles Wilson came to Texas in 1837. He lived in Brazoria and became district clerk in 1845. He served in the Third Legislature, was a member of the Senate from November, 1851, to February, 1852, and served again in the special session of the Fourth Legislature. He died at Gonzales in 1861. *The Handbook of Texas*, Vol. II, p. 92.

[27]Leonidas, king of Sparta, led the soldiers against the Persians in the battle at Thermopylae in 480 B.C. With 6,000 Spartans, Thespians, Thebans, and other Greeks, he faced the 200,000 Persians in the narrow pass. He held the Persians for two days, until a Greek traitor disclosed the pass across the mountains. *The World Book Encyclopedia* (Chicago: Field Enterprises, Inc., 1948), Vol. 10, p. 4373.

[28]A. Garland Adair and H. M. Crockett Sr., editors, *Heroes of the Alamo* (New York: Exposition Press, 1975), p. 76.

[29]*State Journal*, p. 262.

[30]*Ibid.*, p. 270.

[31]Elizabeth LeNoir Jennett, *Biographical Directory of the Texas Conventions and Congresses* (No place or publisher given, 1941), p. 92.

[32]*Senate Journal*, pp. 347-348.

[33]Georgia J. Burleson, *The Life and Writings of Rufus C. Burleson*, p. 741.

[34]L. W. Kemp Papers, The University of Texas Archives, Austin.

[35]Here the reporter erred, writing Robertson for Dickinson.

[36]Adah Isaacs Menken became "the international symbol of glamour and of wickedness." Although she was an inferior actress, she received success performing Mazeppa. "Dressed in pink tights, strapped to the back of a horse that clattered over a circular runway extended into the audience, she thrilled the men and shocked the women." She was "the first woman to bob her hair and the first to smoke cigarettes in public." (Dust jacket to *Queen of the Plaza*.) She died in Paris Aug. 10, 1868, and was buried in the Jewish section of Pere Lachaise. Permission from the city fathers of Paris permitted high stone monument in Montparnasse. An inscription carried her name and the line, "Thou Knowest," from Swinburne's "Ilicet." In

1875 the stone monument was removed because it blocked a street-widening project. Paul Lewis, *Queen of the Plaza: A Biography of Adah Isaacs Menken* (New York: Funk & Wagnalls, Inc., 1964), pp. 291-293.

[37]Lots No. 11 and 12 in Block No. 2 in M. Trumble's Plot. Deed Book F, p. 714, Caldwell County.

[38]Transfer deed, Vol. F, p. 719, Caldwell County Records.

[39]S. Ford Trustee release to S. A. Bellis, Vol. G, p. 32, Caldwell County Records.

[40]Vol. F, p. 770, Caldwell County Records.

[41]Deed Book G, p. 101, Caldwell County Records.

CHAPTER SIX
Early Austin

[1]Katherine Hart, *Waterloo Scrapbook, 1972* (Austin: The Encino Press, 1972), p. 9.

[2]*Texas Siftings*, No. 12, 1881.

[3]Deed Book S-286, Travis County.

[4]Deed Book V-430, Travis County.

[5]Deed Book X-121, Travis County.

[6]Deed Book X-556, Travis County.

[7]Katherine Hart, *Waterloo Scrapbook, 1970*, p. 46.

[8]*Ibid*.

[9]Katherine Hart, *Waterloo Scrapbook, 1972*, p. 27.

[10]*Ibid*. See also Mary Starr Barkley, *History of Travis County and Austin* (Waco: Texian Press, 1963), pp. 180, 262. See also Dr. William Copeland Philips' account book in the Archives of The University of Texas, Austin, for details on horses and tracks in Austin during this period.

[11]Deed Record No. 26, Travis County, from the files of Mrs. R. E. Nitschke, Austin.

[12]Book 29, Travis County, from the files of Mrs. R. E. Nitschke, Austin.

[13] Austin *Daily Statesman*, Oct. 17, 1874.

[14] *Ibid.*, Aug. 5, 1874.

[15] *Ibid.*, Oct. 17, 1874.

[16] Deed filed Dec. 29, 1874, from files of Mrs. R. E. Nitschke, Austin.

[17] Austin *Daily Statesman*, Oct. 29, 1874.

[18] *Ibid.*, Dec. 29, 1874.

[19] Katherine Hart, *Waterloo Scrapbook, 1970*, p. 36.

[20] James M. Coleman, *Aesculapius on the Colorado* (Austin: The Encino Press, 1971), p. 57.

[21] *Ibid.*, p. 56.

[22] Mary Starr Barkley, *History of Travis County and Austin*, p. 81.

[23] Austin *Daily Statesman*, Sept. 29, 1877.

[24] *Ibid.*, March 2, 1878.

[25] *Ibid.*, May 2, 1878.

[26] *Ibid.*, Feb. 8, 1879.

[27] Roxanne Kuter Williamson, *Austin, Texas, An American Architectural History* (San Antonio: Trinity University Press, 1973), p. 55.

[28] Austin *Daily Statesman*, Nov. 5, 1879.

[29] *Ibid.*, Nov. 16, 1879.

[30] *Ibid.*, Nov. 13, 1879.

[31] *Ibid.*, Feb. 20, 1879.

[32] *Ibid.*, July 20, 1880.

CHAPTER SEVEN
Austin

[1] *Austin Directory, 1872-1873.*

[2] Deed Book No. 72 and Recollection of Mrs. R. E. Nitschke's father.

[3]Alfred E. Menn, "Susan Dickenson, Alamo Survivor," *The Dallas Morning News*, March 20, 1954, based on an interview with Miss Annie Hannig.

[4]J. Henry Martindale, "Lady of the Alamo," *Texas Observer*, March 11, 1956.

[5]Margetta Jung, "Alamo's Heroine Gave Texas the Battle Cry Heard Over the World," Austin *American*, April 19, 1950.

[6]J. Henry Martindale, "Lady of the Alamo," *Texas Observer*, March 11, 1956.

[7]Mrs. R. E. Nitschke of Austin has a petticoat which belonged to Susanna Hannig, and it bears out the statement that she was huge in her later years.

[8]Mrs. Hannig owned a number of pieces of jewelry—matching bracelets, beads, breast pins, etc. Many of these were passed on to Mrs. Susan Sterling, a granddaughter who sold them when she faced financial problems.

[9]Menn's article in *The Dallas Morning News*, March 20, 1954, based on an interview with Miss Annie Hannig.

[10]R. Turner Wilcox, *The Mode in Costume* (New York: Charles Scribner's Sons, 1944), p. 310.

[11]Joseph J. Schroeder, Jr., editor, *The Wonderful World of Ladies Fashion* (Chicago: Follett Publishing, 1971), p. 93.

[12]Austin *Democratic Statesman*, Feb. 16, 1875.

[13]*Ibid.*, March 7, 1875.

[14]Guy Morrison Bryan was speaker of the Fourteenth Legislature. *The Handbook of Texas*, Vol. I, p. 233.

[15]Walter Prescott Webb, *The Texas Rangers* (New York: Houghton Mifflin Company, 1935), p. 233.

[16]A. Garland Adair, *Austin, Its Place Under Texas Skies* (Austin: Texas Information Service, 1946), pp. 27-28.

[17]Austin *Democratic Statesman*, Feb. 16, 1875.

[18]Margaret Watson, *Silver Theatre: Amusements of the Mining Frontier in Early Nevada, 1850-1864* (Glendale: The Arthur H. Clark Company, 1964), p. 350.

[19]Austin *Daily Statesman*, July 25, 1875.

[20]Maybelle S. Bigelow, *Fashions in History: Apparel in the Western World* (Minneapolis, Minn.: Burgess Publishing Company, 1970), p. 213.

[21]R. Turner Wilcox, *The Mode in Costume*, p. 307.

[22]Austin *Daily Statesman*, July 28, 1875.

[23]John S. Kendall, *The Golden Age of the New Orleans Theatre* (Baton Rouge: Louisiana State University Press, 1952), p. 517.

[24]Austin *Daily Statesman*, July 24, 1875.

[25]Margaret Watson, *Silver Theatre*, p. 344.

[26]Austin *Daily Statesman*, July 25, 1875.

[27]*Ibid.*, July 29, 1875.

[28]*Ibid.*, July 31, 1875.

[29]Katherine Hart, *Waterloo Scrapbook, 1971-1972* (Austin: The Encino Press, 1972), p. 4.

[30]Austin *Daily Statesman*, April 4, 1876.

[31]Capt. William F. Gray, summarizing the fall of the Alamo as told by Joe, Travis's body servant who was released after his master's death, wrote:
    The servant of the late lamented Travis, Joe, a Black boy of about twenty one or twenty-two years of age, is now here.
    He was in the Alamo when the fatal attack was made. He is the only male, of all who were in the fort, who escaped death, and he, according to his own account, escaped narrowly. I heard him interrogated in the presence of the cabinet and others. He related the affair with much modesty, apparent candor, and remarkably distinctly for one of his class. *From Virginia to Texas, 1835: Diary of Col. William F. Gray* (Houston: Fletcher Young Co., 1965), p. 137. See an interesting discussion on the account in Donna Lee Dickerson, *A Typestick of Texas History* (Austin: Department of Journalism Development Program, The University of Texas at Austin, no date given), pp. 29-32.

[32]Austin *Daily Statesman*, April 7, 1877.

[33]*Ibid.*, April 22, 1877.

[34]San Antonio *Express*, Feb. 24, 1929. The same article appeared in *Frontier Times*, April, 1929.

[35]Austin *Daily Statesman*, Feb. 15, 1878.

[36]*Ibid.*, March 1, 1878.

[37]*Ibid.*, March 3, 1878.

[38]Joseph Gallegly, *Footlights on the Border* (Gravenhage: Mouton & Co., 1962), p. 117.

[39]Bernard Hewitt, *Theatre, U.S.A., 1668-1957* (New York: McGraw-Hill Book Company, Inc., 1959), p. 223.

[40]Margaret Watson, *Silver Theatre*, p. 163.

[41]Bernard Hewitt, *Theatre, U.S.A., 1668-1957*, p. 223.

[42]Margaret Watson, *Silver Theatre*, p. 388.

[43]*Ibid.*

[44]*The Spirit of the Times*, March 14, 1874.

[45]Austin *Daily Statesman*, March 3, 1878.

[46]Bernard Hewitt, *Theatre U.S.A., 1668-1957*, pp. 224-226.

[47]W. Davenport Adams, *A Dictionary of Drama* (London: Chatto & Windsor, 1904), Vol. I, p. 383.

[48]Joseph Gallegly, *Footlights on the Border*, p. 117.

[49]Bernhard Hewitt, *Theatre U.S.A., 1668-1957*, p. 226. Slightly rephrased.

[50]Austin *Daily Statesman*, March 3, 1878.

[51]*Ibid.*, March 5, 1878.

[52]*Ibid.*

[53]Jack Keasler, ''Tenoxtitlan Yule Is Texans' Delight,'' Austin *American-Statesman*, Dec. 17, 1972.

CHAPTER EIGHT
The Alamo Remembered

[1]Herbert Molloy Mason, Jr., *Missions of Texas* (Birmingham, Ala.: Oxmoor House, 1974), pp. 71-72.

²Joseph Gallegly, *From Alamo Plaza to Jack Harris's Saloon* (The Hague: Mouton, 1970), p. 27.

³Alex. E. Sweet and J. Armoy Knox, *On a Mexican Mustang* (Hartford, Conn.: S. S. Scranton & Co., 1883), p. 291.

⁴Henry Barclay Andrews was born on the island of St. Thomas, West Indies, the son of English citizens named Barclay. His father died, and his mother moved to Texas, where she became the wife of Judge Edmund Andrews, who adopted the three children and gave them his name. Henry B. Andrews was educated at Yale University and entered the mercantile business. After reading law with Elisha M. Pease and after being admitted to the bar, he was named attorney of the Galveston district court. He later served in the Texas Legislature and entered the railroad business in 1868, when he became general freight and passenger agent for the Galveston, Houston and Henderson line. He was appointed by Governor R. B. Hubbard one of three commissioners to represent Texas at the World's Fair Exposition in Paris. *The Handbook of Texas*, Vol. I, p. 47.

⁵Walter Raleigh Richardson, ordained Feb. 23, 1862, was the first native born Texan to become an Episcopal clergyman. After serving as rector of St. Stephen's in Huntsville, he became rector of St. Mark's in San Antonio. When St. Mark's was designated a cathedral, Richardson was named dean. Of him, Dubose Murphy wrote, "Although not considered an eloquent preacher, Richardson was a faithful and diligent pastor and exerted great influence in San Antonio. He was much interested in the esthetic side of worship and raised the music of St. Mark's to a high standard. He also did much of the wood carving and interior ornamentation of the church."

⁶San Antonio *Daily Express*, April 28, 1881.

⁷*Ibid.*

⁸*Texas Siftings*, Nov. 12, 1881.

⁹Donna Lee Dickerson, *A Typestick of Texas History* (Austin: Department of Journalism Development Program, The University of Texas at Austin, 1971), p. 98.

¹⁰Austin *Daily Statesman*, Nov. 10, 1881.

¹¹*Texas Siftings*, Nov. 12, 1881.

¹²*The Handbook of Texas*, Vol. I, p. 22.

¹³E. A. Masur of Lockhart wrote L. W. Kemp, Aug. 24, 1938, that "many a time, she (his sister, Mrs. W. S. Vogel) helped dress

the wound in the calf of Aunt's leg.'' The letter is in the Kemp Papers, The University of Texas Archives.

[14]San Antonio *Express*, Feb. 13, 1883.

[15]Austin *Daily Statesman*, Oct. 14, 1883.

[16]*Ibid.*, Oct. 9, 1883.

[17]*Ibid.*

[18]San Antonio *Express*, Jan. 7, 1890.

[19]Austin *Daily Statesman*, Jan. 6, 1890.

[20]San Antonio *Express*, Jan. 7, 1890.

[21]Austin *Daily Statesman*, Jan. 7, 1890.

[22]Curtis Bishop in ''Susannah Dickinson, the Alamo's Forgotten Heroine,'' *Texas Parade* (January, 1964), and Frank X. Tolbert, *An Informal History of Texas* (New York: Harper & Brothers, 1951), p. 105.

[23]E. A. Masur and his brother Joe ran a hardware store in Lockhart. Their grandfather was Joseph Masur, Sr., who came to the United States from Germany with his wife and children. They settled at Lockhart to be near relatives, the Hannig family, which had immigrated earlier. Mary Starr Barkley, *A History of Central Texas* (Austin: Austin Printing Company, 1970), p. 79.

[24]Ferdinand C. Weinert, who had been county judge of Guadalupe County, served in the 21st, 31st and 33rd Legislatures. *The Handbook of Texas*, Vol. II, p. 876.

[25]E. A. Masur to Boyce House, Sept. 26, 1945, in Boyce House Papers, The University of Texas Archives, Austin.

[26]In a letter to the Lockhart *Post-Register*, a copy of which appears in the Louis W. Kemp Papers, The University of Texas Archives, E. A. Masur on July 22, 1937, says Hannig ''positively frowned down on anything that would connect his wife with past historical events.''

[27]E. A. Masur to Boyce House, Nov. 6, 1945, Boyce House Papers, The University of Texas Archives, Austin.

[28]Weldon Hart, ''Mother of Alamo Monument Is Due After 65 Years,'' Austin *American*, April 2, 1948.

[29]Austin *American*, March 1, 1949.

Index

162

163